Life

at Performance Level

Curtis Zimmerman

Applause

"Curtis Zimmerman has the rare gift of combining humor and insight. A year later, he is still being quoted here at Vera Bradley!"

Barbara Bradley Baekgaard
Co-Founder & Chief Creative Officer, Vera Bradley

"Zimmerman's message is phenomenal. Our performance level has increased tremendously and we are seeing results through our changed attitude and productivity... Meaningful information to improve management and leadership skills."

Stephane Zaharia
General Manager, CuisinArt Resort & Spa, Anguilla

"*Life at Performance Level* helps break down communication barriers, energizes the team, and encourages individuals to take ownership of not only how they are living their personal life but also the role they are going to play in their professional life."

Matt Spyers
CIO, Ralcorp Holdings, Inc

"Far exceeded our expectations! Prior to the event, I offered two movie tickets to anyone who wasn't blown away and I am still holding those tickets."

Bradford D. Beldon
President & CEO Beldon Roofing Company
Young Presidents' Organization

"We are living the dream here! It has been a year since Curtis spoke and his message still resonates with the team and the company. The morale and culture has been extremely positive and we are highly motivated and able to face challenges together based on the tools and tactics Curtis laid out for us."

Keith M. Kamalich
Vice President of Sales, Tura L.P.

"Curtis has worked with Florida State University for nearly ten years and has spoken to around 150,000 people on our campus. I continually speak with students and family members who have adopted his charge to be the stars of their own lives, fail successfully, and stop depending on old scripts that limit personal potential. Zimmerman's message and energy reenergizes our staff and holds us accountable for the important role we play in helping students maximize their potential."

Patrick M. Heaton
Assistant Dean of Students, Florida State University

Life at Performance Level

First edition

For information about special discounts for bulk purchases, please contact Curtis Zimmerman Group at 513-229-3626.

Designed by Integrate/ www.integrateinc.com

Edited by Chris Milligan, Melissa Schuler, and Diane Tenaglia

Layout by Aimee Sposito Martini

Manufactured in the United States of America

Curtis Zimmerman Group
7577 Central Parke Blvd. Suite 217
Mason, OH 45040

www.curtiszimmerman.com

513-229-3626

ISBN – 13: 978-0-9772017-1-6

ISBN – 10: 0-9772017-1-6

Noah, Mirabelle and Oliver,

I wrote this for you.

Foreword: Nate Cooper

Author's Note

Introduction

How does a performer's idea translate to a person's life? What does it mean to live *Life at Performance Level*? Great performances begin with an idea and are crafted, refined, planned and constructed until that original idea becomes a more perfect version of what the creator had in mind. This is called Performance Level.

Too often, dreams are taken for granted. They are cast aside as being unimportant. But our dreams, our vision for what our lives could be, are the most important aspect of living. How can you craft your dreams and make them reality? Are your dreams the destination or the journey?

Write Your Script 27

Every choice, every decision, and every action we take as performers is based on a script. Identifying the scripts in your life is a way of identifying the control we have. How do the scripts we follow impact our lives? Is it possible to rewrite old scripts?

Determine Your Role 39

The most fundamental aspect of staging your show is deciding who the main character is and inhabiting that role. In a world where too often people feel lost with regard to who they are, you must realize that you control your show: who the star is and what they will become. What are the first steps in designing and deepening your character?

Star Profile: Rick Murrell 56
The Blind Man and the Razor

Act with Passion 63

Passion is what carries us further. Remaining passionate despite resistance is crucial to being able to grow and change, to inhabiting a new role. Is there a right way to fail? Can dropping the ball be the best thing for you?

Light Your Stage 73

In a theater, lighting is everything. It focuses attention or draws it away; it shows the audience what might be coming and helps develop characters by emphasizing or deemphasizing their importance. How can you control the light in your show? How can light provide focus and expose possibility?

Design Your Set & Costume 83

A performer's surroundings—the space they inhabit, the props that fill that space—are essential elements of a great performance. A character's wardrobe can make an impression long before a line is said. What do our sets and wardrobes say about our characters?

Cast Your Show Wisely 93

Co-stars and supporting roles can make or break a performance. If they are supportive, they make the show better. If they are poisonous, they will destroy the show. What role does typecasting play in our show? How does our capacity for growth relate to how we cast our show?

Star Profile: Dr. Robert Evans 104
A Question of Priorities

Find an Acting Coach   111

Performances are crafted, not made, and performers
develop their craft by always being ready to learn.
What role do mentors play in a great performance?
How can we learn from others without giving up
who we are?

Expand Your Repertoire   121

Does a performer who never stops learning
have an advantage over those who have
mastered a particular skill? What do a mime
and a software engineer have in common?

Project Your Voice   129

In the theater, projecting your voice means speaking
in such a way that you can be heard at the back
of the room. In life, projecting your voice means
acting according to a set of scripts that helps
others recognize your character. How can you
project your voice without saying a word? What
do you think of when you hear your own name?

Do Your Own Stunts   135

How does Richard Branson relate to a teacup? What
stories can our scars tell? People who do their own
stunts are able to balance risk and reward. They
understand there can be no reward without risk.

Opening Night   151

> The curtain must go up and when it does, great
> performers know that they can either be excited
> or afraid. Which one depends on preparation?
> How can you out-work stage fright? What do
> soccer balls, pregnant women and a trumpeter
> have in common?

Take a Bow   163

> There is no such thing as a self-made person. There
> is also no reason not to enjoy taking a bow. What
> secret do great performers know about embracing an
> ovation? What relationship do pride and ego have?

Become an Acting Coach   179

> You spend your whole life building, your whole
> life becoming the master of your show. And
> once you attain it, the best thing is to give

it away. What does teaching teach us about learning? Why the role of acting coach will be the most meaningful part you'll ever play.

There are props to move, costumes to change, changes in lighting and casting. Often the timing of smooth transitions is the key to a successful show.

Now you know what it takes to produce a great life, only one question remains—are you ready to live at Performance Level?

Foreword

In a small community within a relatively small town, you never know when you're going to have an encounter—a chance meeting that will influence your life.

I had an apprenticeship of sorts with Curtis. He took me under his wing and shared the lessons he learned from mentors in his life. He became my mentor, and even more, my friend. He helped me to understand that a performer is never satisfied with their act. A real performer is constantly learning—from experience, from teachers, from other performers.

Curtis helped me sharpen my focus and realize that physical comedy was the right direction for my life. I followed that direction around the world, performing on stages large and small from New York City to Armenia. I set my sights on becoming a performer in Cirque du Soleil, the pinnacle, in my mind, for a physical comedian and performer like me. And I remembered his lessons about failing successfully when I was rejected—twice. I also remembered what he taught me about success when I got the call saying I had gotten a role in Cirque's show "Love" in Las Vegas.

I've been lucky to have a lot of great influences in my life—people and performers who have helped me craft my show. I feel particularly lucky to count Curtis among them. He taught me that if you enjoy life, share your gifts and remain open to new ideas, the show is yours for the taking.

Living the Dream,

Nate Cooper
"The Fool on the Hill"

When I was 11 years old, while walking through the Old Towne Mall in Torrance, California, I saw a mime performing. I was instantly mesmerized. The robot routine was, to that point in my life, the coolest thing I had ever seen. They call it stalking now, but every day for the next three weeks, I followed the mime around the mall. At the end of those three weeks, I gathered all my courage and told him I could do what he did. I told him I had been practicing. Looking back, it was lucky that he was a real person. Had Tommy McLaughlin been something other than that, he probably would have told me to scram, to quit bugging him, but he didn't. He let me show him my robot routine and, when I was done, he asked me to come back the next day.

When I came back, he had the mall management gathered. He told me, "Show them what you showed me yesterday." I did my robot routine and when I was done, the management team looked at me and said, "So?" Tommy stepped up for me. He told the managers that he wanted to develop my skills, to teach me. He wanted them to hire me. They said, "But you're the best mime in LA! Why would we hire some kid off the street?" Then he did something amazing, something I hope everyone who reads this book will have an opportunity to do. He led the managers away. He took them out of earshot. He was firm. He told them, "This is the way it's going to work. You are going to pay him five dollars an hour and take it out of my pay." They shrugged and walked away.

Tommy McLaughlin saved my life that day. He started my career. Every day, for the next year, he taught me. He made $5 an hour less without telling me or anyone. His influence was immediate and it continued through the years, through opportunities and performances. He was a real person. He showed me what it meant to be real. This book is about being a real person.

For the next 30 years, I traveled the world, working at first as a mime, then more broadly as an entertainer. I've seen places I never could have dreamed of and it was all because of Tommy. Were it not for him taking an interest in me and putting himself on the line for me, I never would have met my wife. I never would have gotten out of a difficult early life. I would not have become the man I am today. I have Tommy to thank for that and I thank him every day.

This book is a collection of principles that have guided my life. I guarantee if you act on these principles, your life will change in profound ways.

Among this collection are profiles of people I have met over the course of my career, while traveling and speaking. These people are proof positive that anything is possible, that any dream can be achieved. Their stories are placed between chapters to remind us of our capabilities. These people get it. They exemplify what I hope everyone takes away from this book.

They exemplify *Life at Performance Level*.

Introduction

I want you to imagine something. An image. A stage, an empty stage. No props, no actors. No set design or stagehands scurrying behind the curtains. Just an open space with a single spotlight beaming down through the darkness, waiting to host a magnificent production.

Imagine you are a director, and you can fill that stage with whatever you want. You can choose the story and write the script. You can cast the characters and design the set. You can select props and costumes. You are in control.

Ask yourself—what would you do if you had the power to bring that stage to life? What would the production you create be about? What show would you present to the world?

The fact is, that stage is your life. You do have the control to stage your own show, to be the director, the producer, the scriptwriter, and most importantly, the star of whatever show you have in mind. You have limitless possibility. You have the ability to create the ultimate show, the best story played out by the best actors, the best production designed by the only person who knows exactly what it is you want—you.

William Shakespeare once said that "all the

world's a stage," and he was right, but he did not go far enough. We are all in command of every aspect of our own production. We are the show makers with a quintessentially human capacity to create our own lives, to change that which merits change and celebrate what we cherish dearly.

We all start off with this fully lit stage. But from the moment of our birth, outside influences—parents, family, school, work, friends, mistakes, and successes—begin to pile up, darkening our stages slowly. They darken our stages without our consent. They wrest control from us as directors and producers, players and stars. They twist our scripts and manipulate our sets. And we allow them to do this. We allow the influences of our lives, the outside factors and inward complicities, to force us to stage a substandard production.

These factors also create a basis for our story. Whether we grew up in a loving, supportive household or under the harshest of conditions, these experiences play a role in plot and character development, both good and bad, positive and negative.

It is our right to change the things we want to change, our responsibility as humans to look at the quality of the production we are staging and decide for ourselves what needs to be changed. We have a duty to ourselves and those who love us to stage the greatest production we have the capacity for;

to move from the humblest of community theaters to the bright lights of Broadway and share our story, our script, our characters with the world.

This is Life at Performance Level

Performance Level is the highest, most polished degree of excellence an artist can achieve. Performance Level is the reason you show up early for rehearsal and leave late, it is what drives you to continually rewrite your script and agonize over casting the right players for roles in your production. Performance Level is not the embodiment of perfection but the culmination of hours, days, years spent practicing, spent refining your craft. Performance Level is the act of striving toward a better, more developed life with the goal of meeting your own aspirations, achieving your own vision.

This book is about living your life right now—this instant. It is about taking control and looking at life the same way creators of great shows look at the elements of their vision as pieces of the whole and then seek out a way to meld them together so that the sum of their efforts vastly exceeds the total of its parts. This book, based on my experiences as a performer and a flawed human trying to improve my own life while helping people find the courage and insight to improve their own, is about seeking that higher level of achievement in your life, that level in which you bring the house down every day—Performance Level.

What this Book is NOT

It seems everywhere I go, I see promises from speakers and authors and self-help gurus. "Just follow my simple eight-step plan, and you will be rich and beautiful and the object of jealousy for everyone you know." I see these books and I laugh. Four Steps to this. Nine Steps to that. The truth is that in your life, you will take millions and millions of steps on your own. You stumble. You run. You take small steps, great strides, baby steps, and even steps backwards. You do not need more steps.

Don't expect that in the following pages you are going to find the path to happiness. I can't hold up a map and show you the route to take to fame and fortune and glory. No one can. And to be honest, fame and glory are not for everyone. Leave the promises of fame and fortune to late-night infomercials. This book is about being real.

As a speaker and author, as a human being, I hold no illusion about my ability to change your life. I can't. What I can do is help you realize how much power you already hold. I can give you a new script, a new way of looking at your life that will help you find your own path to success, however you define it.

In this respect, *Life at Performance Level* is not

your typical self-help book and I am incredibly proud of that fact. The world does not need another one of those. This book is about helping you help yourself by giving you knowledge you can apply and resources you can draw on as you stage your own show. I know you are aware of the saying "knowledge is power." That is a lie. Knowledge is not power. Knowledge applied can be powerful, but knowledge for knowledge's sake is called trivia. You didn't buy this book to have more trivia or knowledge that you'll never apply. This book is about applied knowledge, knowledge you will be able to apply to the real world, your world, the world you are going to create.

There is a lot of me in this book, though very little biography. Rather, this is the culmination of the things I have learned, the things I have witnessed in those who have taken their lives to Performance Level. Think of it as a guidebook, a series of insights to be taken, considered and applied in your own life. It is a framework for intent, for action, for rethinking your potential.

I want you to imagine that your life is not the series of actions you take on a daily basis. It is not made up of friends, family and coworkers, but of co-stars and actors playing supporting roles. You are both the star—the person standing front-and-center in every scene, and the director—the person standing offstage creating a vision for a better show. This is a mindset. As we move forward, I want you to keep these images in the back of your mind and remember that no one is invested in the success of your show as much as you are. No one knows what you are willing to give to stage the perfect show. No one has as much interest in reaching your Performance Level as you do. It's time to start taking action.

USE YOUR IMAGINATION

FULLY COMMIT

EMBRACE EACH MOMENT

BE BRAVE

ARRIVE WARMED UP

SAY IT WITH ENTHUSIASM

PAY ATTENTION

BE WILLING TO SACRIFICE

ACT NOW

DELIVERY IS EVERYTHING

BE IN THE MOMENT

DEVELOP A TALENT FOR WORKING

LIVE THE DREAM, FOR REAL

I am living the dream. I really am. I have a successful career as a highly sought-after speaker. I am a devoted, faithful, and loving husband and an equally devoted and loving father to my children. I have had successes and opportunities that have taken me around the world as a headlining performer aboard prestigious cruise lines. I have been named Variety Entertainer of the Year at Universal Studios Hollywood and performed at Caesars Palace. I have a deep and gratifying faith and have authored or co-authored several books. Fortune 500 companies like Disney and Procter & Gamble have invited me to speak to their employees, as have the United States Air Force and hundreds of colleges and universities across the country. I am blessed in so many ways. I bring this all up because it has not always been so.

I just gave you my resumé, but more importantly there is something called my "real-sumé" and often, it reads very differently. And so may yours. I want you to remember, I share this not because it's unique, but because everyone has his or her own story. Real life happens to everyone.

I grew up on food stamps and welfare in Los Angeles, the kind of childhood many people only hear about, let alone experience; a childhood devoid of a whole lot of hope or expectation. Witnessed from the outside, I can understand why someone might not think I would ever amount to much. My family life was in constant turmoil. My mom was married six times, and I do not share a last name with any of my four siblings. We moved 37 times before I was old enough to move out on my own. Sometimes at the drop of a hat, sometimes days before Christmas. There was more than one day when I went to school only to come home and find our house packed up, ready to move.

"Real life happens to everyone."

I had learning disabilities and health issues, which had me in and out of the hospital most of my childhood. Also, thanks to dyslexia, it was not uncommon for me to open a report card and see nothing but Fs. I was in special-ed classes all the way through school.

But I realized from a young age that if I ever got out, it wouldn't be because someone swooped down to save me. I would have to be saved through my own actions, my own initiative. So, as much as I don't like to dwell on my childhood, I have that ragged beginning to thank for helping me understand that potential and success start with a state of mind; that being successful means being present enough, aware enough to recognize opportunities and grab them when they come.

I didn't do it on my own, of course. My show has had a lot of bit players, acting coaches, and co-stars over the years. I have shared scenes with amazing people. But I've also been willing to cut those people out who took away from my show. I don't use my childhood, my rough upbringing, as an excuse, but as a launch pad. Because when you start at the bottom, the only place you can go is up, so long as you are willing to do what it takes to go anywhere.

If I had ever been the kind of person to make excuses, I would have had plenty of opportunity and ample material to do so. But I am not. I refuse to. I refuse to gloss over my failures or put too much stock in my successes, because I know that both are important steps along the journey and mine has been a great one so far. I have achieved things I would never have thought possible, if not for the important lessons you'll find in this book. I have maintained a wonderful marriage for more than 20 years. I own a home and in it, my wife and I work hard to provide a nurturing, supportive, stable environment for our children. I can smile and tell you in all honesty that I am living the dream, my dream, the dream I have for a richer, more fulfilling life.

Not Blind Optimism

Why mention this? Because it is important that we establish from the onset that this book is not theory or pretty sounding metaphors strung together to give you false hope. It is not blind optimism. I have no time for blind optimism. And I don't have the patience for it, even if I had the time. I am not here to blow sunshine your way. I am not here to offer you the promise of a better life. I'm here to help you make that promise to yourself.

I am here to tell you how I did it and how I help thousands of others. How I changed the paradigm of a poor kid growing up with few opportunities and even fewer advantages to being a successful entrepreneur, speaker, and father who commands—and gives—respect from peers and love from family members. So let's get that straight right now. I live in the real world, where people can be cruel and conditions can be harsh. I live in a world where millions go without food or love and where the strongest survive.

And so do you.

And because you're reading this book, you too are already living the dream—at least compared to many who share our planet. For one thing, you can read. In this country alone, nearly 40 million people are unable to read a job offer or utility bill, according to one United Nations study. In sub-Saharan Africa and some areas of the Middle East, the illiteracy rate is as high as 50%. One in two people are unable to understand any form of written language. It is truly astounding. Another thing to be thankful about is the fact that you were able to purchase this book at all. A study from the UN indicates that nearly 3.5 billion people subsist on less than $2 per day. And this is in the 21st century, not 50 or 100 years ago. So, if you paid $20 for the thing you are now holding, a sum that took you a few hours to earn, you spent 10 to 20 day's pay for a majority of the world. So even if you don't feel like you have maximized your potential, these are just a few examples of why you have reason to be happy.

If you need further proof that you are already living

the dream, turn on the television news for 20 minutes. If you are not on it, then your life is truly a dream compared to a good majority of the people in the world. Think of a place like Darfur, where war and violence are a part of everyday life for everyone, including young children. Imagine that you inhabit a world with no concept of convenience stores and delivery pizza, but instead a rather clear idea what senseless slaughter and bloodthirst look like. You may be inspired to thank God out loud that you live the life you do.

"Living the Dream"

What would you say if I were to pass you in the hall and casually ask, "How are you doing?" or "How are things going today?"

You don't need to answer that, because I am nearly positive you would say something like "fine" or "good" or "alright." And you would do so without really thinking about it. You would give me an automatic answer that you have not considered and, more than likely, don't really mean. Why? Because you have been scripted to do so. We'll cover scripts more in another chapter, but it helps to know that the way you answer the question can be telling.

Whenever I am asked how I am doing or how things are going, I choose to say, "I'm living the dream." And it is because I really am. For not only all the reasons I listed above, but also because I am working toward an even greater promise in my life. I'm working toward an even brighter, bolder tomorrow and that gives my life purpose.

Everyone is bound to have a best day in his or her life. Maybe it is the day you win the lottery. Maybe it is the day your child is born or you get married. The 2008 Edition of the CIA World Fact Book cites the average life expectancy for Americans: 78.14 years. That works out to 28,540 days. In that batch there is bound to be one day above all others when everything just seems to be falling into place. When someone asks you how you are doing on this day, it should be automatic that you are able to answer that you are "living the dream."

Conversely, everyone is bound to have a worst day in his or her life. The day their parents pass away or when a child is hurt in a car accident or some other catastrophe strikes. If someone asks you how you are on this day, it would be foolish to say that you are "living the dream," because surely your dream does not involve pain, grief, and suffering.

What Does Life at Performance Level Have to Do with Living the Dream?

What is your dream? Well, for starters, your dream is yours. Maybe it is a dream of owning your own business or achieving a certain position in a company. Maybe you aspire to greatness in the arts or sports. Maybe your dream is to be the best parent, spouse, or friend you can be. Whatever the specifics of your dream, understand that it, above all else, is the reason for your show. That dream is the purpose of your production and the goal you strive toward. Achievement is only a small part. The striving itself is as important as the dream. I have met master performers who have played the same role in the same production day-in and day-out for years, yet they never get bored. They stay in the moment and never lose focus, because they know they are only as good as their last performance and that every performance can be better. They never stop improving. It's not about landing the role or taking a bow, it's about being on stage. The work. The dedication. That's where you find fulfillment.

The Challenge is Tuesday

So, the challenge of Living the Dream and Living at Performance Level is not whether you can stay on top of things on your best day or let go on your worst. The challenge is Tuesday. Not this Tuesday necessarily or next Tuesday or last Tuesday. But every single one of those 28,540 average days that fall between your best and worst. Can you find it within yourself to go a little bit farther, to raise your energy 10 percent more? Can you dig deep and pull yourself out of the humdrum of the middle of the week in order to remain vigilant in pursuit of your dream?

The answer is yes, and this book will show you how.

But in order to do so, you need to alter some of your behaviors. You need to change your preconceived notions about what you are capable of doing. You need to rewrite your script and recast your show, redesign your set and change your stage directions. That is what *Life at Performance Level* is all about: adapting your circumstances and habits in order to put yourself into a better position to live your dream.

It may not be easy. Things in life worth achieving rarely are. Making the changes you need to in order to get to where you want to go will require hard work and a sense of urgency. It may require difficult choices like recasting your show and eliminating the people in it that are poisonous to your character. Often these characters, these players are people we feel close to—a loved one, a relative, a friend or a spouse. It may require a hard look at your own character—your traits, your habits, your beliefs— and adapting them. There are a myriad of things that we will cover that you may need to change. It is very important now to determine whether your dream is really worth chasing and if you are capable of rewriting your show to achieve that dream.

Which brings us back to how we answer when someone asks how we are doing or how we have been. A good test of your readiness to embark on your new production is to change your script here. Can you commit to changing your response for a week? Do you think you have it in you to pay attention enough to ignore the standard responses, the ones that come automatically and without thought? I certainly believe that you can. But if you don't think so or if you are afraid to tell people that you are living your dream when they ask, then you are probably not ready for the content contained in these pages. You can always put this book down now and pick it up again when you are ready to take action.

That's the thing about Living at Performance Level; you have to be willing to attack your life, to sing at the top of your lungs every single day in order to realize the change that you seek. At first it will seem artificial; it will feel like you are faking it, but eventually it won't. It's the "as-if" theory. If you act as if you are successful then guess what? With lots of hard work this type of action eventually will lead to success and you will be "living the dream."

Own Your Show

This has nothing to do with empty affirmation or pipe dreams. This is about perspective, a new way of looking at your life and realizing you have the power to change your limitations and your goals. But first you have to realize you have that control, you have to take ownership. Everything else in this book is hollow if you don't truly understand that you own your show.

> *"Everything else in this book is hollow if you don't truly understand that you own your show."*

You have the control to write the scripts of your life. You, and you alone, hold the pen. Don't allow others to dictate your script to you. Instead, be the author of your show, be the editor of your scripts. Take the time to read them—those actions, those beliefs you have about your life—and examine whether they help or hurt your production. If they help, reinforce them. If they hurt, cross them out and write new ones. In the end, your scripts are the things you control. The way you act, the way you feel, the meaning of your beliefs, these are all scripts. And none of them are permanent. You just need to take the time to read them over, the wisdom to examine them and the strength to rewrite them when needed.

Not all of them have to be big. Not all changes and rewrites mean throwing out the whole book. Sometimes all you need is a small change, an edit here and there. The size of these changes does not reflect their importance. Sometimes the smallest changes make the biggest difference. And there is no script change more powerful than the first one. Because that first rewrite is the most important one of all.

Director's Notes   *For the next week, any time someone asks, "How are you?" or "How are you doing?" stop, think and reply, "I am living the dream!"*

Remember, delivery is everything. Say it with enthusiasm.

THE AMERICAN DREAMER

Roger wasn't meant to live in a big house in southern Virginia. He wasn't meant to find a career in the U.S. He wasn't meant to be here at all. Statistics will tell you that.

Roger Villarreal is the American dream. It's not just that he is living the American dream. He embodies it. He gives it life. If you were to paint a picture of what America represents, what qualities define this nation and make it a shining beacon in the world, what you come up with would look like him. The famous poem by Emma Lazarus that is borne by the plaque on the Statue of Liberty, "Give me your tired, your poor, Your huddled masses yearning to breathe free, The wretched refuse of your teeming shore. Send these, the homeless, tempest-tost, to me: I lift my lamp beside the golden door," reads like his autobiography, his "real-sumé."

"I believe that God blesses me for what I do and for what I have become," he says, his Latino accent colors his words like creamer in coffee. His humility, his willingness to give it all up to God, and to tell you that so much of his story owes to forces beyond his control, makes him all the more impressive.

Roger's life started off like many others in Nicaragua. He was poor. Really poor. Poorer than most Americans dare to imagine. He was one of six, three boys and three girls. At only seven years old, Roger was thrown out of the house by his father to fend for himself with the rest of the street urchins. Today, he doesn't talk about why, nor does he talk about ever having reached the point of forgiving his dad. But there he was, on the street. At an age when most American kids are learning to read and going to school five days a week, Roger was homeless and begging for what he needed in order to survive.

For fourteen years that instinct kept him alive— shoeless, ragged, poor, and tempest-tost. But even at a young age, he had a will to push on, a vision for a better life, even if he couldn't fully understand it.

"I used to walk two or three times a week to the American Embassy in Managua. I walked a mile, a mile and a half, just to watch the flag wave in the breeze," he says. And the way he says it is like poetry, as if he's trying to paint what he sees in his mind with words. "I was living out of garbage cans, sleeping in a park, and I would watch that flag in the wind and wonder what it was like to be part of what it represents."

He can't tell you exactly what it was about America that drew him. He admits he didn't know much. But there was an instinct, something innate like a sixth sense that kept drawing him back to the embassy, to that flag, to that vision of something else: something better, something he couldn't quite visualize or put into words. And then an opportunity came by, an opportunity he nearly missed. It was a newspaper ad for Royal Caribbean Cruise Lines, a want ad written in English. He didn't know much English. "Just enough to be dangerous," he says. But it was enough, apparently, to recognize an opportunity when it came along.

"They were looking for general labor. General labor I could do, even without an education," he says. And this became his first official sale: the product was himself. Royal Caribbean was his ticket out of the slums, a new role on a new stage.

He worked hard. He kept his mouth shut and learned all he could. He learned English. He learned his job. On the maiden voyage of a new ship from Norway to the Caribbean he impressed the chief steward with his work ethic. He was promoted to cabin steward. At the first opportunity, he went ashore and found the American Embassy. He applied for resident status so he could find out what it meant to live under the flag he had spent so many afternoons watching in the breeze. He applied and waited. He waited four and a half years, working constantly, learning, and absorbing. And when after four and a half years at sea he was finally granted permission to go live in America, he did so without hesitation and without a plan.

"I remembered growing up watching the show *Bonanza*," he says. "I went to Virginia because I had been hearing about Virginia City [the Nevada location on the show]. I had no education in geography. I was a fan of Michael Landon. He was my hero. I thought if I could get to Virginia and tell him my story, he could help me out."

And so he went to Virginia and got a job working in construction. It was hard work and not regular. He put on roofs and painted. After awhile, he found an opportunity selling Electrolux vacuums. He became a salesman. But this was the South in the late 1970s, and there weren't a lot of people who looked like him, who sounded like him, who had his coffee-creamer accent. "I got paranoid," he says. "I kept thinking people were looking at me and thinking bad things."

In 1980, he got his GED. Around that time, he entered a 90-day training program for using computers in the production of textiles. For most, it was a hard program. Roger mastered the work in 30 days. For 13 years he worked in the textile industry, doing what he had always done, working harder than everyone else and mastering every new challenge. Then he was unjustly fired. Once again, he had to start over. He heard about a sales opportunity with Clayton Homes, the country's largest maker of manufactured homes. He applied.

"At first, the general manager would have nothing to do with me," he says. Six months later, they called back, but the job slipped through his fingers. The third time he applied, he got the job. In the 18 years since, he has been salesperson of the year, won awards for being a $1-million producer, and won the Circle Award, which goes to the top salesperson for the quarter. He's won the Circle Award 29 times. Twenty-nine times in 72 quarters—that's 40% of the time. The man who once slept on a Nicaraguan park bench was making more money than he could have dreamed, accomplishing more than his humble beginnings would have ever predicted.

"I became an American citizen on September 27, 1987," he says as if it were yesterday. He still celebrates that day, like a second birthday. His voice cracks when he talks about where he came from and especially, where he is now. "I am a very emotional person."

He has never been back to Nicaragua. He doesn't

want to be confronted by it. His parents are dead. His brothers were killed by Sandinista rebels. His sisters live in Florida, but the connection is only occasional. He has a family of his own—wife and children. His oldest daughter was a cheerleader in high school when she took a mission trip to Panama, a country in many ways similar to Roger's native Nicaragua.

Roger has never tried to hide the poverty of his childhood, but he doesn't dwell on the details either. While his daughter was in Panama, she wrote him a letter. For the first time, she had witnessed profound poverty, the worst possible poverty, his kind of poverty. "Dad, I understand everything now," she wrote. She saw how hard it must have been for her father to survive. She imagined the courage it must have taken to dream of something better.

Roger Villarreal is the embodiment of America. He is the definition of this country. When we see the stars and stripes, we should think of Roger. Every one of us is represented by that flag waving in the breeze. We are all like Roger, living our American dreams.

Roger has always lived at Performance Level. Although he never found Michael Landon, what he accomplished through dedication, focus, and faith is proof positive that the American dream is alive and well and living in a big house in Virginia, with a rewarding career, and a loving family.

STOP REHEARSING YOUR LIFE

TIMING IS
EVERYTHING

LEARN ALL THE RULES BEFORE YOU BREAK THEM

YOU WILL FORGET
YOUR LINES; IMPROVISE

KNOW YOUR PART

YOU CAN PLAY ANY ROLE

DON'T BE AFRAID TO BE FUNNY

KEEP IT SIMPLE

DO EVERYTHING WITH INTENTION

HAVE AN IRON WILL

UNDERSTAND THE PLOT

WRITE YOUR
SCRIPT

How much of your day and your behavior is already predetermined? Are you reacting based on your past experiences? Try to think specifically. What patterns have you fallen into? What behaviors would you like to change? Or discard all together?

What if I told you I could teach you how to juggle three balls in under five minutes? You'd probably think I was just kidding or I was like the guy in those late-night infomercials promising domestic bliss for just three installments of $19.95 plus shipping and handling. Maybe you tried juggling once when you were younger and weren't immediately able to get the hang of throwing three balls in the air and catching them, one at a time, with regularity. Maybe you have never tried, but you assume you lack the dexterity or hand-eye coordination to make it work. Either way, you are skeptical of either my ability to teach you or your ability to learn, or, perhaps, both.

Why? What is it about your previous life experience that makes you automatically assume that you can't learn to juggle? Or fly a plane? Write a novel? Make a million dollars? Eat fire? What has happened in your life that causes you to limit yourself in such a way? What is it that makes you think I can't teach you?

Scripts

These limitations, these thoughts that you "can't now, so you will never be able to" are old scripts. They're the parts of us that tell us "no." They create automatic responses to certain things without regard to whether or not those responses are based in current reality. We all have old scripts and they are, indeed, very powerful. Here are some examples: I'm too old to... I can't afford... I'll never have a relationship like... I'm not good enough for... I don't have time to....

In the last chapter, we saw the example of how changing the way you answer a simple question, "how are you doing?" can be a positive first step toward living your dream. Before, you would give me an answer that you had not considered and, more than likely, didn't really mean. Why? Because you have been scripted to do so.

Scripts are very powerful, though not often considered forces in our lives. Scripts are ingrained into the ways we behave from an early age. And they can be stifling and empowering, good and bad. A bad script might make a person believe that suffering through working five days every week at a job they don't really enjoy, but are being well paid at is somehow the right thing to do. A good script or a new script might lead that person to pursue a career that they really love and, in return, allow them to make more money. An old script might make a person believe that they can never lose weight because they tried seven different diets unsuccessfully in ten years. A new script would empower that person to make changes in their lifestyle and script that will lead to lasting weight loss.

> *"Scripts are very powerful. They can be both stifling and empowering."*

I altered my script. I wrote a new one to reflect the actual state of my life. Instead of mindlessly blathering that I'm fine, or that things are fine, I made an intentional decision to change my attitude. Even if the person asking is doing so out of a habit or common courtesy, I rewrote my script to give them an earnest response and found that doing so is an ever-present reminder of how much control I really do have.

How does changing the way I respond to a common question like, "How are you today?" relate to whether or not you can learn to juggle three balls in under five minutes? What does learning to juggle have to do with changing your life? Well the answer to both of these is simple, and it has to do with Simon Says.

Think First Then Do

I love Simon Says. In terms of schoolyard games, I rank it right up there with kickball. And what I love about Simon Says is that it teaches us to think before we act. It teaches us to be *response-able*. No, that's not a misprint. Being *response-able* is different than simply being responsible. Being responsible is taking out the trash when the can gets full and putting ten percent of your paycheck into savings. Being *response-able* is acting with intention and purpose. It is slowing down, even slightly, to consider the consequences of the things we do before we do them. And trust me—I've been playing Simon Says with groups of hundreds, even thousands of full-grown adults for more than a decade—it is not as easy as it seems.

The basic rules of Simons Says are simple. Take a group of people and elect one of them to be 'Simon' for the round. That person gives a series of commands—lift your right leg, touch your nose, raise your hands—that the other players are to follow, but only if they are preceded by the phrase "Simon Says." So, "Simon Says raise your hands," should prompt all the players to raise their hands while a command of "put your hands down," should elicit no response at all. Every person who responds to a command that isn't preceded by the command "Simon Says" is therefore out and must sit down. Easy enough, right?

I have had a lot of fun playing Simon Says all over the country in my years as a speaker, with groups of all kinds including college students, corporate leaders, and more than 20,000 airmen in the United States Air Force. The first few rounds seem to eliminate masses of people and by the time we get to the fifth or sixth round, there are usually just a handful of people left. And these people are always the hardest to get out. Is it because they are somehow more naturally gifted in the game? Are they former professional Simon Says players? Doubtful. What makes these people more difficult to eliminate is their ability to respond to the command given, their *response-ability*. These people think about everything they are told and decide whether or not to react. Instead of absentmindedly throwing their hand in the air or taking a step back with their right leg, they pause to be sure that the command was given in the proper fashion. Simon Says throw your hand in the air, Simon Says take a step back.

And whether the people in that final, most difficult

group to eliminate are corporate officers or janitors, they have an advantage over others who are just beginning to rewrite their scripts. It's because they are able to stop and think before they act. We all need to transfer this skill to our everyday life and stop just reacting to our relationships, to work, and to our old scripts.

When I challenge everyone in the group to give a more thoughtful answer the next time they are asked how things are going, I'm not surprised to find that the people who do well in Simon Says are also those most likely to remember to say they're "Living the Dream." They are the people eager to evaluate their old scripts and make a conscious effort to improve them. The only way to change is if you're willing to stop and think before you act.

Scriptwriting

If old scripts limit us, new scripts enable and empower us.

I was hospitalized 27 times before I was 9 years old with seizures, anemia, and a host of stomach problems. Paramedics came to my house almost every week. And when it was really bad, I was admitted to the hospital. No one could diagnose my illness.

I had EEGs, EKGs, bone scrapings, body scans, and all sorts of tests. I remember flashing lights in a black room, an attempt to induce a seizure. I remember the doctors considering the idea of a blood transfusion. Because of my anemia, I received regular shots of iron, one of the most painful shots a child can receive on a regular basis.

Admittedly, my odds of getting the best treatment were low as we were on government aid and moving several times each year. All this meant that I was seeing many doctors at numerous hospitals. My doctor was whoever happened to be on call in the emergency room.

When I was 16, having been in and out of the hospital continuously, I met what you call a leader and what I call a real person, who happened to be a doctor. He kept me in the hospital, refusing to let me check out until he figured out what was wrong. One morning, he picked up a plate of pancakes from my bedside tray. "You'll never eat these again," he said with a smile. "We've figured it out. You have Celiac disease." Celiac is an often misdiagnosed, rare condition that prevents the digestion of gluten. He told me that from there on out, if not getting sick was important to me, I would never eat wheat for the rest of my life—ever. Seriously, EVER!

So from the moment of that diagnosis to this very moment as I type these lines, I have not eaten wheat. No pizza, no pasta, no beer. Really—no beer. I share this story because it illustrates how a medical condition that I had absolutely no control over forced me to rewrite my script for the rest of my life.

One day, after delivering my message to a company that manufactures in-home, old-fashioned popcorn-popping machines I was approached by a very large man, who was probably seven inches taller and a good deal thicker than I am. I have to be honest, for a moment I had no idea whether I should hold out my hand for a shake, use it to cover my face, or quickly open the emergency exit door.

This man, it turned out, was not there to pound me into the ground, but to share with me that he had just decided to rewrite a script that he had been acting for far too long and one that could eventually cause him a load of trouble. He reached into his back pocket and pulled out a tin of chewing tobacco and handed it to me. "That's my wheat," he said. "And I'll never touch it again."

I have no idea whether or not that man stuck to his new script, but I think we all have moments when we finally, if suddenly, decide to make the changes we need. I have spoken with recovering alcoholics who describe their moment of clarity, that moment of hitting bottom, when for whatever reason they recognized it was time to change their ways. A close friend told me about the moment he decided that his career was not the right one, that it was doing nothing to help him live his dream, even though he was making a good deal of money at it. Money should not be the motivating factor for happiness for him or you. Rather, money should be a reward for the pursuit of it.

Are there things that you do, habits that you know you need to change? It doesn't have to be as dramatic as drinking or drug use. Maybe it is a tendency to rush phone calls with loved ones so you can get off the line sooner. Or maybe it is the habit of checking your e-mail or texts while someone is trying to have a personal conversation. Whatever it is, you need to know that it is not too late to change your script.

Old Scripts

Think about your old scripts, things that you've used in the past as an excuse or a crutch to not make your dreams come true. If you allow other people's

> *"If you allow other people's limiting beliefs about you and your potential to hold you back, the only one who becomes crippled is you."*

limiting beliefs about you and your potential to hold you back, the only one who becomes crippled is you. We all know people who spend their life re-reading old scripts. They will tell you about the horrible thing that happened to them nine years ago. I'm telling you now, it is time to get over it and it is time for you to start writing your new future. The point is to learn to take control of your words and your actions, to be *response-able*. When we take ownership of our scripts, we are able to change them forever. So the next time you are about to react, stop and think before you act. Not only will you win at Simon Says, you will win at the game of life.

New scripts can do a lot more than just improve your future; they can change your past. Today is tomorrow's past. Tomorrow is the past for the day after that. That man who handed me his tin of tobacco changed his past because the next morning, he went from being a life-long user to a former user. He literally changed the definition of who he was. So when I say that scripts are powerful things, it is not just their power to change the present (how we respond, how we act in the moment), but also the future (where we will go and how we will get there), and eventually the past (how we've become the people we are now).

 Director's Notes *Write down a negative script that you are committed to changing. Your timeline for change starts now. Remember, all change happens in an instant. This is that instant.*

DEFINE YOUR PASSION

DON'T BE A DIVA

DON'T TAKE YOURSELF TOO SERIOUSLY

YOU ARE NOT YOUR RESUMÉ

EMBRACE YOUR
CHARACTER

BRING YOUR PERSONALITY

STAR IN
YOUR LIFE

READ THE SCRIPT

LIVE TRUTHFULLY

WATCH A MASTER PERFORMER

DETERMINE
YOUR ROLE

When creating your new show and filling your new stage, it is vitally important that you spend time thinking about the most important element of your production: the main character. Because you are, among other things, the star of your show. The main character is you or more to the point, the new you that is about to debut on this new stage.

You are probably beginning to envision this new character's development: attributes like profession, passions, family life, body type, particular skills, and so on. But you are left with the challenge of figuring out just how to embody those characteristics, particularly if you do not currently possess them. The key is to study the best practices of those who have already achieved success at Performance Level.

Stand Center Stage

Let's start by focusing on strengths and what you are truly passionate about. Let's stop focusing on weaknesses—you'll only achieve mediocrity in something that you're not suited for. Let's take your natural skill set and bring it to the next level— truly mastering not only something that you're interested in, but something you can do better than most. Focus on your strengths and stop worrying about your weaknesses. If we bring our strengths to the stage, we'll amaze the audience every time.

To have an amazing life, you need to be willing to stand center stage with all the lights on and feel proud of the hard work you've put into this skill or behavior. If you could be an expert at anything, what would it be? Don't be afraid to become an expert. Now examine what you're truly passionate about. Your passion is what will take you to the outer edge of your limitations. It will push you to examine other people and what they've done and given in their lives to reach the success level you're looking for. There is no one in this world knocking on doors handing out thousand dollars bills. The way you create wealth in your wallet, in your spiritual journey, and in deep long-lasting relationships is by studying those other "actors" in your show and following their best practices. One warning: just because you appreciate one aspect of a person, does not mean that you need to take on all of the characteristics of this person. The goal here is to take the best character traits and incorporate them into this superstar called "you."

Are you prepared to change what you and others think when they hear your name? That

"Are you prepared to change what you and others think when they hear your name?"

is a huge question. Say your name to yourself right now. What are your thoughts? What do you want to think? Great actors act from the inside out. They exude their character's traits and define who they are by their actions. They never worry about the character they played in their last play.

Your New Show

Everything you've done up to this point is an old production. Now it's time for your new show.

It is important that you learn to distinguish ideals from achievements, opinion from method, and also how to decipher best practices from the whole of someone's life. Uncle Mark might be divorced three times and bankrupt, but he managed to lose 40 pounds when he was 40 years old and kept it off for five years, so what can you learn from him?

These people are not role models or mentors. These are merely people who achieved something you want your new character to achieve. These are people whose practices you can learn from and use to help establish your own, but you cannot follow their path exactly and expect things to work out the exact same way. Though you need to learn from these people, don't take their experiences as the one and only way to do things.

Think about those late-night commercials that promise wealth if you just follow a plan of no-money-down real estate investing. Doubtless the person who created that program did, in fact, make a fortune buying properties and flipping them or renting them out, but what was the economic climate like when they did that? Did they purchase these run-down homes in an area of a particular city that was on the verge of rebirth? What about interest rates and their own assets? There are too many variables in something like real estate speculation for someone to say authoritatively that their way is a guaranteed way to get rich. Nevertheless, it is the way they became rich.

So what do you do? You interpret. You analyze. You sift through and pull out the pieces that make the most sense to you. You understand how other people's methods lead to success and you extrapolate how you can apply those lessons. Warning: If someone tells you his or her way is THE way, then you should run away. There is no such thing as THE way. The goal is to find out the keys to their success and see how they may fit into your script.

The people you choose to learn from don't have to be famous, nor do they have to be people you know or would ever meet, but they should be someone whose habits and experience you can access. If it is someone in your family, interview them. If it is someone at the gym or at work who you don't know, talk to the people who know them—their trainer or coworkers. Seek out this knowledge to begin building the background for your character.

Read the Script, Know the Part, Inhabit the Character

Change takes time. There really is no such thing as an overnight success. Reaching the point where you are living at Performance Level takes dedication and daily discipline. That's why it is important to think of the character you want to ultimately become, to set goals for who, where, what you want to be and when. Goals are tangible; you can track your progress. When I tell people I am living the dream, what I am really saying is that I know where I am and where I am going. I am in the process of achieving the thing I want to become and that I will eventually reach my goals and make my dreams come true. If you haven't set goals recently, I can help you set them with my free goal-setting workbook on curtiszimmerman.com.

As you are developing your new character, some things in your life may need to become unbalanced before you find your new balance. You may need to lose your footing in order to gain new ground. My wife Michelle and I were married 10 years before we had our first child. We each had our own careers, our own way of doing things. Our life at home was established. When we cleaned a room, it stayed that way until we messed it up again. We went to the theater and concerts; we got together with friends. There was a certain balance in our life. And then came Noah.

When Noah was born our life was thrown out of balance. (Michelle's life in particular was thrown out of balance.) She focused on being a mom, on learning what it meant to be a mom. Theater outings, evenings with friends, and the clean and orderly life we had built and grown accustomed to went away. Instead, we had to focus on the addition to our family and learn how to be parents. In time, we began reintroducing elements of our life-before-Noah into our new one. In time, we learned to balance time with friends and time at home, to enjoy the things we had always enjoyed and find enjoyment in this new experience as well. We found a new balance and our lives were richer for it.

Your New Character

There is a downside to writing your new character. There will be people in your life who resist the idea of change. Whether they are your friends, coworkers, parents, spouses, or children, there will be people who consciously or subconsciously, try to sabotage your evolution into your new character.

The fact is that people have certain expectations of who you are. They have roles that they cast you in for their own productions. When you make it known that you are upgrading your character, that you are making a change, there is certainly potential for intimidation and insecurity on their part. Fear of change is even more powerful than change itself, if you allow it to be so. It can cause problems in even the most stable of households, through no one's fault.

If you want the supporting players in your show to accept your new character, invite them into the process. In the work environment, these changes can be equally unsettling to those who have certain expectations of you, your performance, and your aspirations. Some people may resent the longer hours you work because you've decided you want a promotion. You can't be worried about your coworkers' egos or insecurities when you change your character. Nor can you be worried about their success. It is time for you to focus on your show and your show alone.

Imagine being in your workplace. Imagine that each one of your coworkers has a balloon. The balloon represents professional success. If you try to bounce your balloon in the air and worry about helping everyone else keep theirs in the air, then eventually some are going to hit the ground. But if you practice, if you concentrate on keeping your balloon in the air so long that it becomes second nature, that success becomes a way of being, then it is reasonable to think that every once in a while you can reach over and help a coworker keep theirs aloft without letting yours fall. But you can't do that until you've got a good handle on your own responsibilities, your own success.

"Only by focusing on improving your own character can you really, truly help someone else."

Only by focusing on improving your own character can you really, truly help someone else. If someone else's balloon strays, you can bounce yours higher and tap theirs back to them, then return to keep yours in the air. Lifeguards are taught that the most important life they save is their own, because if they don't focus on keeping themselves alive, then they will never be able to save the lives of drowning swimmers. It's not greed or self-centeredness to believe that being the best character you can be will allow you to help others improve theirs.

If you don't possess it, you can't give it away.

For all intents and purposes, my mom was a "crazy-maker" when I was growing up. She was married six times, had five children with four different husbands and constantly surrounded herself with drama. I love her very much—she's my mom—and I would gladly give five lifetimes to help save her. But the fact is I don't have five lifetimes. Just like you, I only have one. I need to make sure that the life I have is stable and positive before I can begin to think about changing hers, or else I will end up being drawn into that world of drama and turmoil, regretting that I didn't act on making my character the best it could be when I had the chance.

Although you cannot become your new character overnight, you need to make changes today that get you one step closer to being that character tomorrow. Begin the process of becoming that character in small ways every day. You're more likely to become that character if you take its traits one at a time. This is how an actor inhabits a character.

Inhabiting means developing the habits that you see as essential to the character you want to evolve into. Actively and purposely adopt the methods of speech, costumes, and mannerisms until they become natural to you.

> *"Inhabiting means developing the habits that you see as essential to the character you want to evolve into."*

Remember to act 'as-if'. It is a process of immersing yourself into the role so fully that you continue to display those characteristics long after the theater has cleared and the audience has gone home. By fully inhabiting your character you are writing new scripts, you are tossing out your old scripts—the habits that have left you short of achieving your goals. A conscious, planned effort to adopt these new habits, these new characteristics, will help us take those crucial first steps to becoming the character we want to become

Beware of Being Miscast

My transformation from performer to speaker was not easy. Change like this seldom is. And a lot of people, no matter how badly they ache to make a transformation, find excuses as to why they can't.

I knew I wanted to become a speaker and doing so would require my learning from other speakers. I had neither the time nor the budget to traipse across the country, going to presentations or taking part in seminars by Tony Robbins. I was hard-pressed to be able to afford to buy a lot of other speakers' books and videos. But you know what I did have? A library card. I drove tens of thousands of miles a year and checked out audio books by the dozens and listened to them all while driving between bookings as a performer for three years. I put the best in a separate pile on my passenger seat, and those were the books I purchased with my limited resources. I devoured their content. I analyzed their delivery. I got a master's degree in speaking from the driver's seat of my car.

Too often in life we are tied to careers and situations we don't enjoy simply because of the benefits they offer. How many unhappy accountants are there who have foregone the life of a therapist or teacher or something they really want to do simply because they were afraid of giving up their salary? In turn, how many people can't get their dream job as an accountant because someone else has it? I saw a bumper sticker once that read, "No one's last words were ever 'I wish I had accrued more equity.'" And there's something poignant about that. What good is having the dream house and cars and comforts if you see them not as a reward for following your passions, but rather as the reason you have to work?

Think about your new character's passions. What makes this new character get up early and go to bed late? What will make you say with enthusiasm "I am living the dream"? Living at Performance Level means being driven by what you do and making your profession or vocation something you are proud to say you have done. It's the pot of gold at the end of the rainbow, the Super Bowl ring after the big game, the standing ovation after a world-class performance.

Traveling the country for all these years, I have discovered (at first to my amazement) that the most successful people, those with the most comfortable living, the biggest bank accounts, and the most fulfilling relationships are the ones who are driven to work by passion, not reward. For them, being able to do what they love is their job. It is so singularly gratifying that the money, the cars, and the houses are all secondary. Are you following your passions? Do you get up every day with a burning desire to do your job? If not, it is time to change that, to rewrite your script and find your way toward true, satisfying success.

Beware of Typecasting

A few years ago, I was scheduled to do a keynote presentation at a university in Utah. I boarded the plane and flew across the country. When I landed, I was greeted by a young man with more than a few piercings. He was there to greet me and take me back to campus for my talk. On the drive over, we talked about his major, his goals, and his dreams.

"What do you want to be some day?" I asked him.

"I will be President of the United States," he said.

I extended my hand and told him that I wanted to shake his hand now, because when he one day does become the President, I wanted to be able to tell my friends that I had met the leader of the free world when he was in college. It would have been easy for me to assume that a pierced college student from Utah has little, if any, chance of ever becoming the President. It would have been easy for me to typecast him. When we typecast, we operate from a set of assumptions that have more to do with the limitations we have encountered than with those a particular individual has. It may well be that that young man will become the President, despite his appearance. I have no idea, because I have no idea whether he is willing to do whatever it takes to become President.

Wouldn't it be horrible if he only became a Senator? The problem with how most people set goals is not that they set them too high; it's that they set them too low—they want to be realistic. I'm telling you right now, you should try being unrealistic for a while. You might be amazed what the world will give you.

One of my role models, Walt Disney, was never accused of being realistic. Realistic never invented anything.

It's the same with any typecasting. Whether we assume things about a person because of the shape of their body, their skin color, their age, or job, any time we make snap judgments based upon incomplete information, we are limiting that person in our own minds. And if we express those limitations, we open the possibility that they may believe us and thus, limit themselves.

> *"Realistic never invented anything."*

Typecasting others means limiting their development in your show. Allowing others to typecast you can be equally as limiting. But typecasting yourself based on one small incident or one minor failure is the most dangerous limitation of all. If you look back on your life in high school and see only the time you were embarrassed in the cafeteria, you are typecasting that part of your life. It's important to also remember that you were named to the homecoming court. So often we typecast ourselves according to what we see as our failures, ignoring our successes.

The key is not to dwell on one without dwelling on the other. Everyone has ups and everyone has downs. The important thing is looking forward while remembering, completely, where we came from. Someone may try to limit you based on a failure. Others may try to lionize you based on your success. This typecasting by others starts with the role you inhabit yourself. If you marry your character to your failures, how will others know about your successes and vice versa? Don't typecast yourself and don't allow others to typecast you by thinking you are only capable of one kind of role. You are capable of so much more.

If you are of a certain age, the character Superman might bring to mind Christopher Reeve and his curly lock of hair determined to retain its place on his forehead. An older generation might think of George Reeves, who played the role on the 1950s television series. It's common for people to associate famous characters with the actors who played them. But what if I were to mention Christopher Reeve first? What would you think? You might remember that he was paralyzed in a horse riding accident, but more than likely you would remember him for his work playing The Man of Steel. Would you remember him as Bob "Bagdad" Freed in *Speechless*? Or what about Richard Collier in *Somewhere in Time*? The amazing roles he played on Broadway? Or that he graduated from both Princeton and Juilliard?

Typecasting is what the doctors and therapists did to me when I was young. I was typecast as a sickly child, as a person with dyslexia, a child of a dysfunctional home. We have all been typecast by people in our past. The people who overcome typecasting are those who can recognize it for what it is—labeling and a crutch.

Some people with Celiac disease let the disease define them. They become obsessed with their diets and driven by what they can't have. They go to support groups to talk through their feelings about something they cannot control. They hand the disease the keys and let it drive. Me? I choose not to let it define me. In fact, I think of it as a trait that makes my character special. I get to talk to the chef of every new restaurant I visit. I get to try foods most people would ignore in favor of another slice of pizza or a plate of pasta. Celiac is a gift, because I am writing the show.

That's the problem with a crutch, if you use it, if you buy into the notion of it, then you are the one who ends up crippled by it. Christopher Reeve never stopped. He became an advocate for research to cure spinal injuries. He became an inspiration to millions around the world.

So, think about typecasting before you walk on stage. How are you being typecast? Are you typecasting anyone in your life? How are you going to prove to the audience that you are capable of playing more than just the character they have seen you play?

Just remember, some new shows deserve a new audience.

Director's Notes *How are you allowing yourself to be typecast? Determine your new role.*

THE BLIND MAN & THE RAZOR

As a teenager, Rick Murrell was an angry young man. He was lost, an outcast among his peers and failing at school. He was living with his grandmother in England, sent away from his home in Kenya by his mother for opportunities he didn't understand.

But that was a long time ago. Meet Rick now and you see a contented man, a successful, affable man in his mid-60s. He's the Chairman of the Board and President of Tropical Shipping and Construction Company, a Fortune 500 firm and the lifeblood for those who live in the Caribbean. He's happily married and when he speaks, he projects an air of satisfaction, accomplishment, humility, and approachability. It's a chance encounter followed by years of dedication that turned that angry young man into the content, successful man of today.

Rick was 14 when he was sent away. He loved Kenya, a land of vast open spaces and sunshine. But Kenya in the 1960s was a land in turmoil and his mother was resolute. She sent him from the place he loved to the cold, dim confines of England.

He was shunned and made fun of as the "new kid from Africa." He felt confused and lost. He ended up last in his class, a social outcast.

Transformation from childhood to adulthood was not going well for Rick and he didn't see it getting any better. However, Rick soon found out that seeing was not nearly as important as feeling. He had no prospects and no hope for anything better, only resentment for leaving the life he wanted behind, and contempt for the one he found himself living. That is until one day when he sat down to watch his favorite news program *Panorama* on the BBC. His mother had instilled a love for the news in him. That curiosity and passion for current events carried with him to England and he developed a liking for Robin Day, the bow-tied anchor of the *60 Minutes* like program.

Rick was sitting on his grandmother's couch. He remembers it clear as day. His grandmother was away, tending to some need for the grocery store she ran. And near the end of a relatively mundane show, Robin

Day announced the segment, which had to do with a blind man and his everyday life. Rick's interest was piqued because his grandmother donated a seeing-eye dog to the blind community every year. She was not a rich woman and the cost was not small, roughly equivalent to $30,000 per dog in today's dollars, but she considered it part of her duty to the greater society.

"At this point, I am angry as hell at life," says Rick. "But that interview was a moment of transformation for me. It changed my life."

In the interview, the man laid out the facts of his life. He was married, had children, and a good job. His family took vacations. He had a home. In short, he had everything he needed in life. He just couldn't see. Almost as a throwaway question, Robin Day asked the man how he shaved. Did his wife do it for him? Was there some secret?

He told Robin, "You know, you don't really need to see in order to shave," Rick remembers. "You just feel. The only thing you need your eyes for is to drive and my wife takes me where I need to go."

Something about that simple, straightforward answer to a seemingly uninspired question touched Rick Murrell, changed him, and flipped a switch inside him. Right there and then, he vowed never to look in the mirror again when he shaved. Shaving blind would become his daily reminder of just how much he had in life—his health, his family, his mind, and his sight. It was to be his daily devotional, his reminder that when you look for opportunity, when you have a positive attitude and are aware of all the gifts you have been given, there is nothing you cannot achieve.

The next morning he shaved by feel for the first time. And though he cut himself badly and had to patch his face with toilet paper, he was resolute. Every morning he tried again and within a week or so he was able to do it without cutting himself. Shortly after that, he found he was better at shaving with his eyes closed than he ever had been looking in the mirror.

The results were immediate. After spending the summer holiday between school years in Kenya, he got on a plane and watched his home country disappear beneath a billowing blanket of clouds and thought, "This is the last time I will ever see Kenya. I'm going to go to America and become an American." At the end of that next school year, he won the award for being the top student in his class—having literally gone from worst to first.

When his schooling was done, he moved to the Bahamas, where he worked for a food distribution company. He took the job because it was geographically closer to the United States than any other offer. While he was on the path toward his dream, he experienced a few missteps and rocky roads.

At one point, he was considering leaving the Bahamas and going back to England, forgoing the promise he had made to himself as a young man. On one particular day he left work at around two in the afternoon to go home and shave. He didn't need to shave because his whiskers had grown since that morning; he needed to shave because he needed an attitude adjustment. He needed to remember that frustrations are temporary, that opportunity is everywhere. He needed to be reminded of the blind man who had unwittingly become his role model, to remember the things he had and the things he wanted in life. He needed to remember how lucky he was, despite the frustrations, despite feeling like he was stuck.

He returned to work and shortly thereafter was approached by the Tropical Shipping and Construction Company. They pleaded with him to stay in the Bahamas and work for their young company. They did everything they could to convince him that it was the right thing to do. Rick shaved a few more times, found his perspective, and in time took their offer because he saw the positive that could come from it, the chance to get closer to his goal.

Now, from his office in Palm County, Florida, Rick Murrell looks back on his career, his life, his climb to the top of the company's ladder and his journey toward his goal. He realizes how fortunate it was that he was in England that day on his grandmother's couch: a lonely, angry young man just waiting for his life to be changed. Having a positive attitude and respect for people and the understanding that everyone has something to offer—these are the cornerstones to his success and the drive that has carried him through an extraordinary life.

He goes to bed feeling lucky and blessed and thankful for the decisions that were made on his behalf, the choices he made for himself, and the opportunities he came across. And in the morning, when he wakes up, he shaves, without looking. He remembers that it is possible—better—to do it by feel.

Rick is reminded every morning when he shaves. He has never grown a beard, never lost sight of his goals. He has never let success go to his head or failure to his heart. Not permanently, anyway.

I found out in the course of writing this book that Rick had only shared this story for the first time with me. I am deeply honored that he would allow me to share it here, with you.

BE OVER-PREPARED

MASTERY IS NOT GIVEN

BUT EARNED

DON'T WORK FOR APPLAUSE

TALENT IS A MYTH

THE SHOW MUST GO ON

DON'T LISTEN TO THE CRITICS

DEVELOP A TALENT FOR WORKING

TAKE NOTES

PASSION SUPERSEDES NATURAL ABILITY

ALWAYS SAY YES

PRACTICE

HIT YOUR MARK

ACT WITH PASSION

Take time to celebrate every step you take toward reaching your goals.

Changing your character is not a sprint. It is a marathon. When you run marathons, you must rely on passion. Natural ability, training, practice, and planning may get you ready, but it's that burning desire that keeps your legs moving into your twentieth mile, that drowns out the screams from your muscles, and carries you through to the finish line. Passion supersedes natural ability every time. It is the

"Passion supersedes natural ability every time."

trump card when the hand is lost. Get passionate about your new character and your new show and applaud every mile along the way. The strides that carry you forward and the ones that trip you up, the small daily successes and the failures. Passion makes you appreciate one and learn from the other.

People without passion, those going through the motions, miss out on their small successes and allow failures to stop their progress. Successful people, people who are living at Performance Level don't think this way. Instead they celebrate their failures just as much as they celebrate their successes. They succeed with perspective and fail successfully.

The Key to Success is Failure

Too many people give up too easily. When confronted by something new, they try a couple of times and without experiencing success, they walk away. They write it off as something they will never be good at, something they weren't born to do. But ability is rarely the deciding factor in success. A person can be born with all the ability in the world, but if they aren't willing to hone their skill, to practice long after others have quit, they will never experience the satisfaction of putting their natural gifts to use successfully.

We have a strange view of failure. We come at it from the wrong direction. We view failure as a stop sign instead of a textbook. Failure is a fantastic way of learning, but you have to be willing to embrace it, to celebrate it and realize that failure is an event, not a person. Failing at something doesn't mean you are a failure as a person, it means you have room to improve.

I have experienced and witnessed failure a lot over the course of my lifetime and career. I know a lot about it. I know that most people do not give

"Failure is an event, not a person."

themselves enough opportunity to fail because they fear it.

An example: I have taught hundreds of thousands of people to juggle as a part of my presentation. When I tell people I am going to teach them how to juggle, the reaction is often pretty similar. They moan or shy away, they tell me they can't learn how to juggle. And I tell them, they absolutely can and that it's not the juggling they are afraid of, it's failing.

But failing is nothing to be afraid of.

I can do some pretty amazing things with juggling balls. I can do some cool tricks. I can juggle with my eyes closed and bounce balls off the walls. I'm proud of that, not because I am egotistical and showing off my natural ability, but because my abilities are a reflection of my willingness to fail. I have failed more at juggling than almost anyone I have ever met. I've dropped tens of thousands more balls than I have caught. But every time, I used that failure for what it's good for—assessing what went wrong, making adjustments and getting right back to practicing.

So when people roll their eyes or tell me they can't learn to juggle, I tell them they need to readjust their relationship with failure. I tell them that of the few things in life that are certain, failure is one of them. And you can either shy away from failure or you can write a new script and embrace it, celebrate it and learn from it.

Readjust your Relationship with Failure

Are you willing to give yourself 5,000 tries—literally 5,000 tries—to perfect an aspect of your show? You need to be, because if you are only willing to give yourself a couple of tries, you won't succeed. You need to be willing to fail 4,999 times in order to achieve that perfect 5,000th attempt. That is the key to success. Ask any of my children what the magic word is and they won't say 'please' or 'thank you.' They will tell you 'practice.' Because practice is the magic word, it is the key that will open any door. Practice is the act of failing, but failing successfully by learning from the times we don't succeed. Practice is where we drop the ball, over and over again and cheer every time it hits the ground. We celebrate the things we learn as a build-up to that time that we try and succeed.

Some people will drop the ball in their career, in their relationships, in pursuit of their goals, and let it eat at them for months. They will allow one failure, one tiny little flop, to prevent them from moving forward. But what does that do? It leaves them going nowhere and feeling bad about it. And all because they don't embrace failure for the gift that it is—an opportunity to learn and grow.

The same goes for businesses and organizations. I speak with a lot corporate executives about how failure is viewed in their organizations. And time after time, the companies that are doing the best are the ones that embrace failure as necessary to innovation and leadership. They understand that if they don't encourage failure, then their competition is going to take away their market share.

> *"Embrace failure for the gift that it is — an opportunity to learn and grow."*

Failing successfully is not just a metaphor; it is the key to success. If you are not failing, you are not growing. And if you are not growing, you are not writing new scripts. And this book is all about new scripts. You should be too.

Celebrate your successes and embrace failure as a

means of learning a better way to achieve your goals. If you didn't go to your scheduled workout today, be sure to go tomorrow, and then take the time to analyze why you skipped that workout. Whatever the reason, rededicate yourself to the big picture plan and stay flexible. Fail successfully and you'll succeed.

Mastery is Possible

I have always been very goal-oriented. It's the way I learned dozens of skills as a mime, magician, juggler, and performer. I would decide that I wanted to learn something and then work doggedly until I not only could do it, but I had mastered it. A perfect example of this determination is how I came to be able to roll a fifty-cent piece across the top of my fingers.

As I grew into my teenage years, I began working regularly as an entertainer and performer at places like Marineland, an aquatic park. Though I lived in LA, getting to work meant a long bus ride across town, since I rarely had the opportunity for a ride. So I decided that if I was going to be sitting on a bus for two hours a day, I was going to use that time wisely, learning to roll coins across my fingers. For hours and hours each week, I practiced, sitting at the back of a crowded bus. And eventually, I had mastered the one-hand coin roll. I had not only learned how to do it, I had mastered it.

Rolling one coin across your fingers is one thing,

but I was not happy settling for that. I decided to learn how to roll a coin across both hands at the same time. Eventually, I mastered that as well, further elevating my abilities. But, I still wasn't satisfied. So, I set about learning to roll two coins simultaneously across a single hand and, eventually, rolling two coins across two hands—four in all—at the same time, a skill maybe a dozen people in the world at the time could claim as their own.

Your Character's DNA

This story is not about my dexterity with fifty-cent pieces. It illustrates the point that people who strive toward building a better character for their production are not content to settle for doing something adequately. Rather, they write into their character something I call DNA, which stands for Do Nothing Average. If you plan to be the star of the greatest production you can set your mind to imagining, then you need to find it in yourself to be extraordinary.

When I was young, I was told over and over again that I suffered from learning disabilities and that implied certain restrictions, a limiting of expectations for what I might achieve in life. Had I listened to the school psychologists or so-called experts, had I allowed myself to be limited by the labels they put on me, what do you think the odds of my writing this book would be? Exactly. Had I allowed the things other people put on me to define me, I would not be where I am today—a trait I think you'll find common in the lives of successful people.

Think of Abraham Lincoln. Had you been a sophisticated city-dweller in the early 19th century and I came up to you and told you that a boy who grew up in a log cabin, reading meager texts by the light of a single candle was capable of writing something as moving, powerful, and enduring as the Gettysburg Address or his Second Inaugural Address, you may well have laughed me out of the room. Yet Lincoln did just that and his refusal to be pinned down and defined as nothing more than some sort of uneducated rube has served generations of Americans, indeed people around the world, for more than a century and a half. He mastered the skills he needed to find success as the character he chose to play.

As you consider, plan, and write your ultimate character, what traits and skills will be a part of your DNA? (Do Nothing Average.) Mastery is not only possible, it is essential if you are going to reach your ultimate goal, which is, of course, to live your dream.

 Director's Notes *Pick a skill you gave up on learning. Fail until you've mastered it.*

LOOK HONESTLY AT YOURSELF

BE BRAVE

USE YOUR SPACE

STAND CENTER STAGE

LISTEN ACTIVELY

STAGE FRIGHT IS COMMON

FIND YOUR LIGHT

IMPROVE YOUR CONCENTRATION

TRUST YOUR GUT

BE ON TIME

FOLLOW YOUR COMMON SENSE

HIT YOUR MARK

LIGHT YOUR
STAGE

There are two kinds of lighting in a theater: house lighting and stage lighting. House lights let you see the whole theater. They help you find your seats and your friends. Under house lights, you can walk up and down the aisles; see the architecture of the theater, the color of the walls. Stage lighting, on the other hand, draws an audience's focus to the stage. The house lights go down, the stage lights come up, and the large open theater becomes smaller, the audience's vision is drawn away from the architecture, the color of the walls, and their fellow audience members. They are drawn to the light on the stage.

Our lives benefit from these two ways to use light. House lights, those that allow us to explore the world around us, are the lights of possibility. Stage lights, those that force us to focus on the characters on the stage, on the voices and dialog, give us an opportunity to take a closer, narrower look at ourselves. Learning how to use these two kinds of light in our lives will help develop our character and open the world around us.

The Light of Possibility

When we are born, the whole world is bathed in light. That is to say that our entire stage is basked in the warm glow of what is known in the theater world as a "general wash." This is because the moment of our birth presents us with infinite possibility. At that moment, we are all capable of anything humanly imaginable. But as we grow older and we begin to write scripts, some of the bulbs that create the general wash, that bath of soft warmth, go out, and our stage begins to reveal pockets of darkness.

As you may have deduced or might soon find out, actors are only as good as the light they are working in. There is no point in working in the dark, since the show cannot be viewed or admired by anyone. So each time we write a script that somehow limits us, that is, each time we tell ourselves that we are incapable of doing something, a little arc of blackness takes over part of our stage. The more we say no, and the more we listen to our limiting beliefs, the more we convince ourselves that those limitations are real. Eventually, we are left with nothing but a small circle of light that limits movement and choices. Although these limitations are self-imposed, to the character in the scene, they are real, insurmountable barriers preventing us from moving freely.

What once had been a completely lighted stage offering boundless possibility becomes something more sinister and severe, a life in which we have convinced ourselves that we cannot do anything but stand in our place and not move around.

> *"A completely lit stage offers boundless possibility."*

Perhaps you feel a bit like this: limited in your choices, held fast to the small space you have left. For some people it is a career that is holding them back, for others it is an unhealthy relationship, either past or present. Either way—or any of a million other ways you can find yourself stuck in such a predicament—the feeling is one of anxiety and, far worse, a complete lack of hope.

But you know the amazing thing about light bulbs? They are connected to a switch that allows you to turn them on just as easily as you turned them off. Don't be afraid to flip that switch. It's not too late to rethink your limiting beliefs, to rewrite the lighting cues in your script.

When was the last time you walked the stage of your life and looked up to see which bulbs were burned out? When was the last time you got out the big ladder, the ladder of renewal, and climbed the rungs with measured steps, gingerly removing a burned out bulb and replacing it with a new one? Sometimes our lights are burned out, not turned off. Replacing those bulbs requires action, a series of steps to bring you back to the light. Some bulbs aren't completely burned out, but they've dimmed over time. And while examining the bulbs that light all parts of the stage, maybe it is time to rethink wattage. Are your relationships lit by 20-watt bulbs? Is it time to shine a brighter light, to replace what's there with a 100-watt bulb? What are the five most important lights on your stage? What part of your life needs the most light?

> *"Maybe it is time to rethink wattage."*

Light Design

Lighting design is one of the most important jobs in the theater. Be the lighting designer of your life, to make sure that as your character moves about the stage, you can be seen from every seat in the house—every aspect of your life is illuminated brightly.

You may not be fully aware of where your character's

lines came from, the ones written in your past that are limiting you today. You may not remember why you walked away from learning to cook, but you can see how that decision has prevented you from becoming a chef. It's like that with any of the scripts you have written throughout your life. The reason you are not a captain of finance is because you made a decision at some point to not study economics. Whether you presumed that it would be too hard or you simply had no interest doesn't really matter. All that matters is that you are not living your life as a financier now. You may be in a crummy marriage because you have a hard time opening up emotionally. Most likely, something happened along the way that prevented you from opening up fully. It might have been abuse you suffered as a child or things you witnessed in your own parents' relationship. You wrote a script that prevents you from ever really opening up again and until you make the conscious decision to rewrite that script, you will be incapable of realizing the intimacy you desire and deserve.

Performance Level is about a lot more than being your best today, it is about preparing the stage and writing the scripts that will allow you to put on the show of your lifetime tomorrow and the day after that and every day until the final curtain falls.

The Light of Examination

The other kind of light common to theaters is the spotlight. This is the brightest light in the rafters, the one that cuts through all others and makes the lead actor stand out among the cast. It can be a harsh light that reveals every flaw, every wrinkle on your face or worn spot in your costume. It can also be a tool that helps accentuate your smallest movement and emphasize the slightest change in expression.

For the purposes of refining your show, we want it to be both. We want it to be 5,000 watts smack on the top of your head and rather than turning from the glare, we want you to stand boldly in the light to face it with pride and honesty. This isn't about being the center of attention; this is about centering your attention on yourself. Honesty is crucial to life at Performance Level. Being open and receptive is how we get real with ourselves; it is how we learn about the negative scripts that hold us back and the positive ones we forget to celebrate.

"This isn't about being the center of attention; this is about centering your attention on yourself. "

It is important as you move closer toward life at

Performance Level that you take time every day to reflect on your progress. Old scripts and negative scripts are not just things from your past; they will constantly be a part of your life. You will develop these limiting characteristics without even knowing it. It might be that you have a bad day at work or you are having trouble learning the new software and you're frustrated. Without knowing it, you will put up a wall, you will extinguish a light on your stage and perhaps without even realizing it you will tell yourself that you lack either the skills or the brains to master something new. This script should be treated like an old one and thrown away. It is vastly easier to deal with a fading bulb than it is to change one that has burned out. By taking time every day to reflect on your progress, you can catch bad scripts before you miss out on opportunities, you can overcome your self-imposed limitations before they do damage.

Embrace Light and Silence

There is something magical about silence. Especially in the media-heavy, distraction-filled times we live in. It seems everywhere you go, the grocery store or in an elevator, you are confronted by noise. And if noise is not supplied for us, we carry cell phones and iPods and other devices that are meant to keep us connected to the world but really rob us of the gift of silence. The area under the glare of your spotlight is silent. That's the magic of light—it makes no noise but reveals so much. Take time every day to sit in silence and reflect on your progress.

Once you get the hang of listening to silence, slowly begin replaying the previous day. What successes did you have? What got you one step farther down the path toward Performance Level? What limited your progress? What scripts were negative? What script are you going to write today? I find this exercise works best in the morning, at the dawn of a brand-new day. You may try it at night before bed, but I find I am either too tired or too wrapped up in what happened during the day to find the right mindset for deep and meaningful evaluation. You may do it over lunch or after you put the kids to bed. But it is important that you make the time for yourself, that you make it a priority to step into the spotlight and examine your character's progress, the scripts you have written and how they relate to achieving your ultimate goal of Living your Dream.

Also take this time to reflect on the world around you, to turn down the spotlight and turn up the house lights. Think about the situation you are in at work, about your relationships and the things in your life that may get taken for granted. Think about what you can do to strengthen those relations, to take advantages of opportunities and make a plan. Write a script to help you explore more fully the potential that exists around you.

When you are comfortable in silence and able to use light to its fullest potential, you'll start to see that the things that limit you—worries, frustrations, limitations and old scripts—are not as powerful as you imagined them to be. And that by focusing both on your character under the spotlight and the entire theater under the houselights, you will find new ways for the two to interact in order to make your show that much brighter.

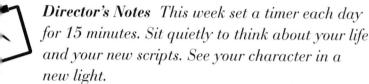

Director's Notes *This week set a timer each day for 15 minutes. Sit quietly to think about your life and your new scripts. See your character in a new light.*

USE YOUR SPACE
DON'T UPSTAGE
PAY ATTENTION
HAVE YOUR COSTUME READY

LOOK THE PART

BE WHAT YOU WISH TO SEEM
KEEP IT SIMPLE
DON'T BE A DIVA
USE YOUR IMAGINATION
DEVELOP A BODY THAT WILL DO
WHATEVER IS ASKED OF IT
LIVE TRUTHFULLY
KNOW YOUR OBJECTIVE

DESIGN YOUR SET & COSTUME

What do you want your set to look like?

Seriously. What do you want your set to look like? Don't tell me how you are going to get it, don't tell me that you do or don't deserve it, just admit right now the things you want.

For some reason, there seems to be a natural tendency for people to lie when they give their answer. Call it being politically correct or sensitive to the plight of others, but for some reason we have a hard time saying what we want.

Honesty is essential to achieving Performance Level in your life. You have to be honest about all the characteristics that make up your character, even when they seem unimportant. Beating yourself up for wanting things is like sitting in a rocking chair—it gives you something to do for a while, but it doesn't get you anywhere. So we have to be honest and embrace the things we desire. We have to be real enough to realize that wanting things does not make us bad people, and we have to have the audacity, the work ethic and the drive to make them appear.

I've wanted things—a bigger house and a nicer car. I'm sure if you're honest, you have too. I also want to pay for my children's educations, to be able to retire at a reasonable age, and have the ability to continue my life-long love of traveling. What's wrong with that? Nothing. That's part of my script. These things are important to my overall production. If the human species never aspired to greater things, we would never have left the cave. Aspiration for greater things has spawned invention and driven innovation.

> *"Aspiration for greater things has spawned invention and driven innovation."*

But let's make no mistake; there is a distinction between aspiration and greed. Greed means wanting things without purpose. Greed is saying that you have to have things for the mere sake of having them. Aspirations are about surrounding yourself with tools, objects, and accoutrements that complement and reflect the nature of your character. Your set, costumes, and props serve to enrich your character's show, not the other way around.

With that in mind, what would you do if suddenly you had infinite resources to invest in your show? What would your set look like? What about costumes? I want you to build it now in your head.

You should realize by now, that I am not interested in the short-term and that Performance Level is about staging your show to the best of your ability and with the highest use of your resources until the final curtain falls.

Sure, you may think you'd enjoy lounging by the ocean, drinking fancy rum drinks out of coconuts for a while. Maybe you could even do that for a year, but I ask, what then? What is it that is going to bring purpose and meaning to your life after the sheen of freedom has worn off? What meaning is that big white house or fancy sports car going to have when they are old enough to need repair? What purpose are they going to serve then?

When you start to consider these things on a deeper level, you begin to realize the difference between shallow thrills and real satisfaction, cheap distraction and meaningful attainment. If your show is to be successful, all the pieces have to work in concert; they have to fall in line to get you to where you want to be. So when you start thinking about how your set and costume serve the greater good and add to your show, it becomes a little easier to admit wanting them.

Your Set

Housing is a multi-billion dollar industry in the United States. Even in the worst years, it is a major force in driving the economy. Housing is also a big part of your show. You may want to live in a nice house in the suburbs because it offers safety, comfort, convenience, and access to quality education for your children. You may want to live in a townhouse or apartment in the city because it keeps you close to the action and allows you the opportunity to experience an urban lifestyle that really suits your character's personality. You may want to live in the country on a farm or in a cabin in the woods because you cherish the solitude and closeness to nature. Whatever your ultimate setting is, it should reflect the character you plan on playing.

The same thing goes with cars and other possessions. If you want to drive a sports car, drive a sports car. If you want to drive a minivan to haul kids to soccer practice, drive a minivan. Whatever the possession, whatever the decoration, make sure it suits the character you are developing.

It may be as simple as burning a scented candle or

having fresh flowers in the house. It may be playing a certain kind of music in the background or having a big table for family get-togethers. It may be a backyard garden or a basement man cave with a pool table and big screen TV. All of these help set the mood, the tone of your show. They enhance the stage of your life.

Let's remember, none of these things will magically appear. We must design them as set designers, piece-by-piece, to create the place we ultimately want to live. We must plan them and take the necessary steps to bring them to fruition. Where we live, our set is a reflection of our character and must be planned accordingly.

There's a fine line between planning and fixation. Do not become so focused on what your set looks like that you don't take action. Make decisions and move toward bringing those decisions to life.

"Our set is a reflection of our character and must be planned accordingly."

Don't worry. You can always make changes as you go along. Envisioning your set—making plans and decisions—is a way of complementing your character's progression, not defining it. If your character changes, allow the decisions you make about set design to change too. But never let your vision for a set dictate the progress of your character. That's what happens when people allow themselves to be owned by their possessions instead of the other way around.

Your Costume

Costumes play an important part in the creation of your show because they help an audience identify elements of your character before you move a muscle or utter a single word. Your costume can work to your advantage, especially in the early stages of working toward Performance Level and Living Your Dream.

Don't take this the wrong way; I am all for self-expression, but sometimes you have to look the part in order to get the part. If you are an actor called in by a director of a play to audition for the role of a father, you are going to show up to the waiting room outside the auditions and find that you are surrounded by a lot of other actors who look an awful lot like you. They are going to have similar body types and hair color, they are going to look approximately the same age and have similar talents.

So what will set you apart from all the other talented actors vying for the same role?

Look, we have all seen the TV shows that give everyday people a makeover, and often they end up looking twenty years younger. You have to ask yourself, is it time for your character to have a makeover in order to feel more comfortable in your new role?

Sometimes we have to look the part. When we go on job interviews, we need to look like a professional. When we meet a new client, we need to look like we're experts. When we play ball with the kids in the back yard, we need to look like we are relaxed and are enjoying the time we are spending.

You don't always have to be the one in the suit or the shirt with the company logo. There will come a time when you can call your own shots. But that time comes after you land the role, after you achieve a measure of

"Is it time for your character to have a makeover in order to feel more comfortable in your new role?"

success and seniority. When people begin to value your passion and insight, you can have more freedom. It may seem as if I am telling you to stifle your creative fashion choices or your ability to express yourself through your appearance. I am not. I am merely suggesting that changing the paradigm, reversing the norms for what is considered acceptable is a lot easier to do when you are the person directing the show than it is when you are the person auditioning for it. Wear the costume. Inhabit the role. And then one day, when you are making the decisions, you can decide how all those actors waiting in the wings should look when they step into your production.

Then again, you might find that dressing the part suits your character perfectly. You might realize that dressing a certain way gives you a sense of empowerment or pride. It all depends on your character, the person you are and the one you will become. You don't necessarily have to abandon your shorts for a suit—the opposite might be more appropriate. It all depends on the role. Either way, it is important now, at the beginning, to project a sense of your character's dedication toward growth and your costume will make a world of difference.

 Director's Notes *Envision your set. Cut out a picture from a magazine and stick it to your mirror. If you own a smart phone, take a picture and make it the wallpaper. Use it as a reminder of the goal you are working toward.*

Open your closet and look at your wardrobe. Does it suit your new character?

DON'T UPSTAGE
COLLABORATE
FOLLOW YOUR COMMON SENSE
SHARE THE STAGE
TRUST YOUR GUT
KEEP AUDITIONING

BE BRAVE

DON'T BE A DIVA
LOOK HONESTLY AT YOURSELF
FULLY COMMIT
BE WILLING TO SACRIFICE
STAR IN YOUR LIFE

CAST YOUR
SHOW WISELY

Have you ever been to a show and walked away thinking it was amazing, but not knowing why? Have you ever wondered why a show with a great script, an interesting plot, and interesting characters came off as flat or unsatisfying?

The answer is casting. Ask any performer, any director and they will tell you that 90% of the magic that goes into making a show a success is casting: choosing the right players for the right roles, balancing each other out, and allowing the star to shine.

In addition to being the star, director, producer, lighting, set and costume designer and writer of your show, you are also its casting director. It is your job to choose a supporting cast that will help the star's performance really shine. Think of some of the best plays, musicals, and movies you have ever seen. How did the supporting cast work to make the production extraordinary? The characters you love and remember probably provided support and love, comic relief, and insight that the lead drew upon in order to take the performance to the next level.

Supporting Characters

Everyone in your life is a supporting character. Friends, family, coworkers, and colleagues all play an essential role in your show. And if you are serious about taking your show to Performance Level, then you need to be as thoughtful, as deliberate in choosing the people you surround yourself with. Supporting players can serve as a valuable resource, helping you realize your dream, and celebrating the steps you take along the way. They can also be a negative influence, a detriment to your progress.

Their presence in your production is completely your choice.

You are the star of your show. You are the only one that will be in every scene in your life. You are the only person who will wake up with you each morning and go to sleep with you every night. You had better like the company! I want you to think about the six or eight people you surround yourself habitually with right now. Do they make your show better? Do they build you up? Or do they drag you into the wings and suck the life out of you?

> "*You are the star of your show. You are the only one that will be in every scene in your life.*"

Poisonous People

We need to give the poisonous people fewer lines and ultimately, for some, we may have to write them out of our show entirely. We may have to give them time to go off and work on their routine so that at a later date, if we choose, they can audition again to join us in that stage of our life. Unless we remove the negative and poisonous people from our stage, we will not have room for the healthy characters waiting to join us in the next phase of this amazing production.

Poisonous characters are not always the ones who abuse you or distract your life with drama. They don't have to be an abusive husband or a drug-addled girlfriend. They can be the people who stand in the way of you rewriting your scripts. They can be the coworker who doesn't want to see you succeed or the friend who only wants to take from you, without giving anything back. Poisonous characters are the ones that you realize, when reviewing your scripts under the spotlight of examination, are preventing you in any way from reaching Performance Level.

Reducing a poisonous person's role in your life may be the hardest thing you will ever do, especially if that person is a relative, spouse or someone whose presence you have grown to count on or expect.

But this is a decision you must consider, for the benefit of your new character.

Re-Audition

We also must allow others to grow and change their roles. You have to allow for the fact that your friend may reexamine their character and realize that they can be more giving, that your coworker may realize they should be more supportive. The amount of refinement a cut character needs to do before they can re-audition is proportional to the damage they caused.

None of us are perfect. If we were, we wouldn't need to rewrite scripts, we wouldn't need to recast shows. We are all on a journey. You are right now. You are making changes in your show in the hopes of making it better. We have to allow others the ability to do the same. There are times when we have to cut characters out of our show or else risk never rising to Performance Level. But if those characters go off and work on their show, if they rewrite the negative scripts in their lives, we need to allow them to re-audition when the time is right.

We have to have the capacity to forgive and the wherewithal to recognize when the time to forgive is not right. It is a difficult skill to master, I realize, but far too important to not consider. And when we feel like we have a true understanding of our production—of every aspect of it—it becomes easier to make those casting decisions.

Great directors know exactly what they want their show to look like and they cast accordingly.

Now, let's focus on giving more lines to those people in your life that bring your show to the next level. Here are a few things to look for when casting your show, a few characteristics to make sure you are choosing wisely.

Look for people who give you the opportunity to speak and listen to what you say. The best supporting actors are engaged in what the star is saying and doing. Great supporting characters lean forward when you talk. They are interested and excited about you. They are willing to go out of their way to help,

"Find people who care about you, not what you can give them."

and you find yourself willing to help them as well.

Find people who care about you, not what you

can give them. There is no ulterior motive. There is no expectation that they can gain from you. Great supporting characters are honest without looking for faults, people you can trust to tell you the truth without brutalizing you for the purpose of building themselves up. They are generous with their support, their love, and their attention. They want to see you succeed in whatever you do.

Different Characters Play Different Roles

Understanding that we have different characters standing on different parts of our stage helps to manage our own expectations when it comes to casting. The people we work with may not be the people we set goals with. The people we marry may not be the people we do business with. The people we interact socially with may not be those we see at church. This is okay, but the opposite is also fine. There's no reason characters can't cross boundaries and support us in multiple portions of our stage. Just recognize that the expectations you might have for the person in the office next door should probably be different from those of the people you want to spend the rest of your life with. Look for honesty, caring, and integrity in all characters, but realize the roles they play differ depending upon their position on the stage.

Be Willing to Share the Stage

Realize that you are a supporting character in other people's shows as well. Sometimes we look for role models, people we can learn from, but often the people we learn the most from are the ones who seek to learn from us. Don't be afraid to allow other characters the opportunity to take a bow on your stage, they will appreciate it, you will appreciate it, and it will give your show more credibility in the eyes of the audience.

Create an Ensemble Cast, Not a Monologue with Extras

The success of your show relies on you not only surrounding yourself with positive supporting characters, but being one as well. Know when to speak up and when to listen, give what you hope to receive, and the production will be the stronger for it. The best supporting characters are those you can call at three in the morning to help deal with an emergency.

"The more people who can count on you, the more you will have to count on when you need them."

The best lead characters are those who will pick up that phone when it rings the other way. The more people who can count on you, the more you will have to count on when you need them. Relationships are about shared commitment to the betterment of all the characters on stage. Learn how to choose those who appreciate who you are, who you want to be, and the character you are growing into.

Finding Your Co-Star

There can be no more important character than your co-star, the person who plays the biggest supporting role in your show. For many of us, this will be our spouse, our partner, or the one we promise to spend the rest of our lives with. Marrying someone doesn't necessarily make him or her an ideal co-star. But the right co-star can make all the difference, ensuring that you will reach the Performance Level you strive for.

I met my wife, Michelle, when we were both working on a cruise ship. I was working as a mime and juggler; she was a singer and dancer. It was, I must say, our very own Love Boat. For one thing, we had a lot in common when it came to our characters and scripts. We both loved performing; we were both adventurous enough to throw caution and sensibility to the wind and work aboard cruise ships. And, as we grew closer and spent more time together—there really is no courtship in the world that can equal the unreality of life aboard a cruise ship—we found that we shared many of the same values and dreams.

We were compatible in a way that belied our backgrounds. I grew up in a dysfunctional home in Southern California, and she came from a solid home in a semi-rural part of Ohio. But despite, or maybe even because of, our differences, we were able to see something in one another that led us to believe that we should continue on this journey together.

Being willing to share the stage in an unending passion to make the other person's show better is one of the characteristics you may find in a perfect co-star. Co-stars do not upstage one another, but are devoted to each other's performance, understanding that they can rely upon one another for support, comfort, and honesty when they are needed most.

If you feel like you are being miscast or unfairly cast in your most important relationship, you need to rewrite that script together. You need to talk to your co-star about the way you are being treated and stand up for your character. You need to work together to change the dynamic. This is natural. This is healthy. If you believe you have been miscast, chances are your co-star is feeling the same thing. There's no such thing as one unhappy person in a relationship. As we grow, we can grow together or we can grow apart. If you find you are growing apart, it is time to stop and reassess the scripts you've created together and write new ones through honesty, give-and-take, forgiveness, and trust. Without trust, no relationship can thrive. And without honesty, there can be no trust.

> *"A supporting character shares the stage, but a co-star shares the spotlight."*

I'm proud to say that my partner is the most honest person I have ever met and that my show is better because she's in it. It does not mean that every scene together is effortless, but it does mean that my production has more meaning and value because she is there. The plot is richer because of the lines and the accountability she brings to every aspect of my life.

The difference between a supporting character and a co-star is that a supporting character shares the stage, but a co-star shares the spotlight and applause.

Director's Notes *Cast your show wisely. List the 6-8 people you surround yourself with. Give more lines to healthy characters. Reduce the number of lines you give to the poisonous people.*

A QUESTION OF
PRIORITIES

Ask any doctor what it takes to get them where they are and they'll tell you it takes years of dedication, drive, and single-minded determination. Ask Dr. Robert Evans about it and he'll tell you about the years of school, tortuous hours as an intern, and even longer hours as a resident.

It's hard to imagine finding time to fall in love and get married, but he did. The woman he married understood his drive and focus in a way most other people could not. That's because she was doing it too.

The Evans got married between their second and third years of medical school. They became chief residents—he in pediatrics, she in obstetrics and gynecology. The hours got even more brutal, but they were working—individually and together—toward a vision. But even the best laid plans, no matter how well thought-out, can be thrown.

The Drs. Evans weren't trying to have a baby. It was one of those happy surprises, but one that would require adjustment. They were two people, two chief residents on the verge. A baby was a welcome addition, but it meant balancing more than work schedules and time together.

For two years after the birth of their son, they improvised. Who will pick him up from daycare? Who will be there when needed? How can we be two places at once? Then, their daughter was born and with her, another year of the circus-like balancing act of aspiration, career, and obligation. Their lives were in turmoil. Something had to be done.

They could no longer make their family fit their careers. The focus and dedication that had carried them through medical school and residency was detracting from the success of their family, children, and home. One of them needed to cut back, to stay home.

"There were nights when my wife was supposed to pick up the kids. But at 4:30 a patient went into labor, and she couldn't leave so we had to change the plans," says Dr. Evans. "The whole thing just became a struggle."

After a good deal of deliberation, they decided the best option was for Robert to stay home with the kids. "We looked at our financials and realized we could get by on my wife's salary. There wouldn't be a lot of gravy, a lot of extra for fun things, but we could do it." It wasn't the obvious choice. A generation ago, no one would have imagined the father staying home. Nor was it easy for a successful doctor to walk away so early in his career after more than a decade of hard work and sacrifice. But the Evans wrote their own scripts; they made their own rules and made a decision based on what they saw as best for their family.

Robert threw himself into the role of primary caregiver as feverishly as he did that of a doctor. He took his son to pre-school and got involved as a room parent. He spent time with their daughter, helping her grow and develop.

"For the first six months, it was great. It felt like there was stability in our household for the first time," he says. But after six months, Robert had fully immersed himself in his new character's role as caregiver, forsaking other aspects of his life. There were times when his wife would work for 36 hours straight, leaving him in charge of the household. He was a parent 24 hours a day and didn't make time for himself.

"I understand now why so many at-home mothers join mom's groups or playgroups. It's to have that adult interaction, that outlet. At the time there wasn't anything like that for stay-at-home dads and I think the mistake I made was not finding an outlet for myself, not doing something for me."

The kids were happy, things were getting done when they needed to be done, but Robert realized that his life was just as out of balance now that he was at home as it had been when he was working. Despite being around his children all day, he was stressed and lonely.

He didn't regret the decision to stay home, but in choosing to make his family a priority over his career, Robert had inadvertently made the decision to exclude himself from those priorities. He had sacrificed his own happiness for stability in the home, and that decision was unsustainable. He could not go on in that way.

Once again, the Evans family deliberated and found a solution whereby Robert could work part-time in order to get the things he needed while still tending to the needs of his family. He would still be the one volunteering at school, the primary caregiver, only this time he'd have the outlet he lacked and a proper balance of priorities.

It was also around this time that Robert and his family found faith as Christians. This added depth to their lives. A newfound faith served to strengthen the Evans family bond and reinforce Robert's decision to put family ahead of career.

It was not enough to simply switch one set of obligations for another. Success is bred from balance. In the 14 years since Dr. Evans made the decision to throw his chaotic life out of balance in order to find a new balance, he has managed to play an active role in raising successful kids while building a successful pediatrics practice—with three offices. He still volunteers weekly in the school, and encourages his employees to make their families a high priority. Schedules are adjusted to meet family obligations.

"My wife gave up her obstetrics practice about nine years ago. She no longer delivers babies and has made her schedule more nine to five," he says. "We're always there for our kids. There is always at least one of us at events and we almost always have dinner together. And I think that has made a difference. Having that stability in the home has made for more confident, well-adjusted kids. They think for themselves. They don't stick to a clique or a certain group of friends. They are good students. They have good heads on their shoulders. I like to think that we had something to do with that."

In a profound and unexpected way, walking away from a medical career to become a full-time caregiver made Robert Evans a better doctor. Had he never stepped back, never stayed home, he may have fallen into a trap that befalls many focused and driven people—they become focused only on themselves. Now, when a parent comes to his office in the middle of the day with three kids in tow and a haggard look, he understands. He's been there. He knows what it's like to feel lost amid a family's needs. Those parents will tell you what that means, to have a doctor care as much about their well being as he does about booking more appointments. He treats the family, not the illness, because he has experienced what it is like to be a parent in need of a personal connection.

Sometimes we have to exchange one kind of chaos for another in order to discover the calm that lies beneath. Success—at work, at home, anywhere—is a balancing act requiring a shift in priorities and needs, aspirations and what you are willing to sacrifice. Finding that balance can be hard. But if you do, success is the result. Just ask Dr. Evans.

FIND YOUR OWN VOICE
ARRIVE WARMED UP
TAKE NOTES
IMPROVE YOUR CONCENTRATION
LISTEN ACTIVELY
COLLABORATE
GIVE YOUR SKILLS AWAY
KNOW YOUR PART
BE ON TIME
WATCH A MASTER
PERFORMER
DON'T WORK FOR APPLAUSE
BRING YOUR PERSONALITY

FIND AN ACTING
COACH

You can spend years studying for a degree, ace every test, read every book, and yet you will not come close to learning as much about your desired profession as you will by spending time with someone who has already mastered it.

That's why when someone tells me they have a degree in this or that, I ask them how much time they have spent actually doing it. You can take all the accounting classes you want, understand all the tax laws ever written, and memorize theories until the cows come home, but you can only be an accountant when you learn how to use that knowledge in the real world.

As I stated before, the saying "knowledge is power" is a lie. Knowledge for knowledge's sake is called trivia. Knowledge applied can be powerful. Indeed, it is learning to apply knowledge that takes a different kind of teacher than the one that typically stands in front of the classroom. It takes a mentor or, as I like to call them, an acting coach.

No Excuses

I never went to college. In fact, I am lucky I was able to graduate from high school. I showed up every day, and I smiled a lot. As a performer, I learned my craft from some of the greatest performers from around the world. I learned about speaking by reading and listening to every self-help and business book I could get my hands on for over three years before I ever gave my first speech. I had mentors like Dr. Will Keim and David Coleman, The Dating Doctor. I learned from these people, I absorbed the hard-fought lessons of their experience, and I can honestly say that I would not be nearly as successful today if I had never met them.

Can degrees open doors? Absolutely. Does having a foundation of knowledge in topics related to your field help when it comes to applying yourself to a career? Without a doubt. Do I expect my children to go to college? You'd better believe it. Do I think it makes you better equipped for a successful career? Possibly, but it is not automatic.

There's a misunderstanding about the educational

process and what a degree means. Formal education is not the be-all and end-all. Achieving a college degree or certificate does not automatically make you an expert. Experience combined with an education is the best baseline for knowledge I have found. When experienced people are willing to share their knowledge with you, it is truly a gift.

By the way, if you are reading this and you don't have a degree, it's not an excuse to limit your character's potential. I have done over 200 new student orientation presentations on college campuses nationwide, and I was never a new student. The only thing limiting you is you and your old scripts.

We All Need Mentors

When I was starting out as a speaker, I approached David Coleman during a conference he was giving, recruiting speakers to be a part of his agency whose main focus was booking speakers on college campuses. He was already a tremendous success, giving more than 150 speeches a year. He had to turn bookings down because he simply was not able to accommodate them all, which gave him the idea of training speakers to deliver his keynote. I went to the conference, but I wasn't interested in delivering his keynote, I was interested in sharing my own message. I approached David after his talk and told him that I would do anything—shoot video, carry bags, anything he needed—as long as he would share with me some of the experience he gained over the years to become a successful speaker in the college market.

It would be impossible to put a value on the amount of wisdom and experience David shared with me and equally impossible to come up with a sum that totals the wisdom I gained from spending two years touring college campuses with Dr. Will Keim. As I grew more comfortable working with these two men, they gradually gave me more and more opportunities. Dr. Keim even allowed me to lead a section of his keynote addresses, where I learned to translate my experience as a professional mime into the ability to captivate an audience of thousands with my voice. While both pursuits involved a certain amount of showmanship and stage presence, they could not have been more opposite. I went from performing without saying a word to performing with little more than words. Talk about a dramatic career change—it was an entirely new script.

More than just watching each of their appearances, I was studying these pros, learning every aspect of what they do from crafting a keynote presentation to meeting with audience members after their program. Like all good mentors, communication and learning was a two-way street with them.

They weren't teachers or sages delivering the same speech again and again—they never settled. They were always working on their presentations and refining their lectures to find new ways to reach their audiences at a deeper level. In return, I shared with them my experience in running a small business, budgeting and, of course, marketing. I had a lot of experience selling a product no one wants. I mean, who ever thinks, you know what we need? A mime.

David, Will, and I opened several successful businesses together over the years, and I remain proud to count them not only as mentors, but friends.

So what does this mean to you as you set about recasting yourself into a new character? Quite simply it means that you should never, ever stop learning. And the best teachers the world has to offer are those who have been there before. So whether you want to be the next great butcher, baker or candlestick maker or the most attentive, best parent your children could be lucky enough to have, my advice remains the same—find an acting coach.

"The best teachers the world has to offer are those who have been there before."

I was fortunate to have two acting coaches that

were willing to take me on the road with them and teach me by letting me witness their shows first hand. But having an acting coach doesn't need to be cumbersome; you don't need to leave your life and take to the open road like I did.

It may be a person at work, a senior manager, a neighbor or a friend. The fact is that you don't have to go to a library to be surrounded by knowledge. There is wisdom residing in every person you pass on the street, every friend, coworker, and relative has something they can offer in terms of experience. That's the advantage of living on this planet. We all have different experiences to draw upon, and we all possess the capacity to teach.

Tips on Learning from an Acting Coach

Having an acting coach or mentor is not about learning to copy exactly what they do. If I had signed up to be one of the speakers that delivered David Coleman's Dating Doctor keynote, I would have limited my ability. I would have been an imitator, and imitators rarely innovate. Instead, I absorbed David's experience and filtered it—breaking things down to understand how the things he did led to success. I could never achieve the same success by repeating his steps. I had to learn and absorb and then apply what I learned to my own situation. I took what David and

Will taught me, blended it with my own experience and ended up creating something new, something unique to me: my own script for the success of my own show.

If a writer wants to be as prolific and successful as Ernest Hemingway, what do you think will help him more: learning that Hemingway was known to write standing up and thus standing when they write? Or understanding how Hemingway used his own experiences as a foreign correspondent for the Kansas City Star to develop the plots of some of his most famous works and then drawing on their experiences to come up with their own plots? The answer should be obvious. So keep in mind that the goal of having an acting coach should be gaining enough knowledge to carve your own path, not just following in their exact footsteps.

"The goal of having an acting coach should be gaining enough knowledge to carve your own path."

Mentors are never perfect. No one is. They did not do everything right all the time, and you won't either. You can learn just as much from their failures as you can from their successes. Be open-minded and listen for the things they would change about the way they did things; listen to the scripts they wish they could rewrite. Often, these will be the greatest lessons they can pass on.

Finally, be careful when learning from an acting coach not to be too drawn in by the advice they share. Take it in, absorb it, chew it over in your mind and then be willing to let it go. Advice and wisdom are built upon the experiences of the person dispensing them. There are very few universal truths in this world, and no matter how certain your mentor may be about something, you get to decide whether or not it fits into your show. Still, even if you do not take the advice they give, be thankful for their willingness to share.

In every step of your progress toward achieving Performance Level, seek out the wisdom of an experienced acting coach and when, at long last, you find yourself in a position to be a mentor, embrace the prospect openly and share generously.

 Director's Notes *This week find an acting coach to share a skill or knowledge to help your new character.*

Do something to make their show better as well.

EMBRACE NEW SKILLS

LEARN ALL THE RULES BEFORE YOU BREAK THEM

TALENT IS A MYTH

HAVE A SENSE OF PLAY

MASTERY IS NOT GIVEN BUT EARNED

DEVELOP A TALENT FOR WORKING

ACKNOWLEDGE THE CROWD

PRACTICE

BE OVER-PREPARED

DEVELOP A BODY THAT WILL DO WHATEVER IS ASKED OF IT

KEEP AUDITIONING

YOU ARE NOT YOUR RESUMÉ

EXPAND YOUR REPERTOIRE

There are freaks of nature in this world. People for whom talent is as natural as breathing, ability is as seemingly abundant as appetite. They are special, endowed with a little bit extra from the Creator, a special gift to get them started in the world. You read stories of seven year-old cellists soloing at Lincoln Center or 13 year-olds graduating from medical school, and you have to scratch your head and say, yeah, that's incredible.

Chances are pretty good that you're not one of those people. I know that I am not. Ability comes to people like us as a reward for the effort we expend in attaining it.

I was invited to a juggling convention about fifteen years ago. At this point, I had been performing and entertaining for fifteen years. I had juggled at Universal

Studios, in television commercials and at Caesars Palace in Las Vegas. I wasn't able to juggle five balls, but I had a very solid three-ball routine to the tune of "Dueling Banjos." I felt pretty good about myself. I got to the venue, and it was everything you would imagine a juggling convention to be. There was stuff flying all over the place—bowling balls, knives—people walking around on stilts, and even a unicycle or two.

I was watching jugglers practice their craft when a young man, about 14 years old and wearing sneakers, jeans and a t-shirt, walked up and stopped right in front of me. He pulled out a black velvet bag, and he opened it, producing five beautiful red juggling balls. I thought, what's he think he's going to do with those?

To my amazement, for the next two minutes, he juggled five balls without a single drop, caught them in his hands and, as if nothing had happened, he put them back in his bag and walked away. In that moment, I knew one of two things had to happen: I either had to kill him, or I needed to rededicate myself to this skill. Needless to say, no one died that day. But let's remember, I had been juggling for 15 years—he was 14 years old. He juggled with such incredible ease and skill that it lit a fire in me. I went home and for three days did nothing but learn to juggle five balls. It had never been that big of a priority to me before—just something I might learn someday. Seeing that young man exhibit his talent made me realize that I could do it, I could write a script in which I was able to juggle five balls. I still recall waking my wife up at two in the morning, screaming, "I did it, I did it. I can juggle five."

I ask you, what is your five-ball juggling routine? What have you written off as impossible? What do you need to rededicate yourself to?

Learn Everywhere

One of the advantages of working in amusement parks and other venues was that there were all kinds of entertainers. Mimes, magicians, actors, jugglers, fire-eaters, you name it. Most of these people were masters at what they did. I would walk around the park, strolling between performances and watch these artists at work. By watching, I was inspired and I knew that I would never be content as only a mime. I wanted to learn magic and unicycling, juggling and sleight of hand. So I would trade people for talents.

In the break room, I would ask the other performers if they would be willing to teach me one of their skills. In return, I would teach them one of mine. In exchange for learning a magic trick, I would teach the magician something about miming. When I wanted to learn juggling, I would teach the juggler a magic trick. I never settled for just learning these skills, I had to master them. I had to be good enough at magic to be a magician, good enough at juggling to be a juggler. And on and on.

So that's what I did. I would learn a skill from a master and work on it over and over until I had mastered it myself. I thought it was curiosity. I thought I was just interested. Then, after I met my wife and moved to Ohio, I began to realize that the extra hours I spent expanding and mastering my act would work to my advantage in unforeseen ways.

Let's say you are planning a festival and you have $600 to spend on roaming entertainers. For $200 you can hire a so-so magician. For $200 you could hire a mime and for another $200, you could hire a decent juggler. But what would you say if you could hire one person who was all three for $500? That was me. Sure, it meant that I had to work extra hard on the day of the booking. I had to do a set, change my costume, and do another. I had to do the work of all three people, but I got all three people's pay. Plus, the organizer of the event didn't have to make the effort to hire multiple entertainers. It worked out for both of us.

This model may seem a bit far-fetched if you work in sales at a software company, but consider how economic swings can have an impact on your job security. For example, say there are five sales people and five people who write software. The company is restructuring and they have to get rid of five people. Who are they going to keep: the sales reps that know how to do only sales or the software pros who do nothing but write software? Or, are they going to keep the three sales reps that have taken the time to learn to write software and the two software writers who have learned the sales process?

The days of being a specialist are over.

In today's business climate you can't do just one thing and expect to get ahead. That is, of course, unless you have mastered that one thing to the point where you are a world-renowned expert. Remember that boy who juggled five balls? He kept working on his juggling and adding to his repertoire. The last I heard he had performed around the world as a leading performer for Cirque du Soleil.

Add New Skills

More likely for you and me, surviving and thriving in this world requires that we keep adding new skills to our character's bag of tricks. And we are constantly surrounded by opportunities to learn new things. Opportunities abound, even at work. Many companies break their employees into teams with representatives from different departments putting their heads together to share best practices. If you work in a team like this as an engineer, for example,

> *"Have a resumé that gets longer every single day."*

you have an opportunity to learn from the marketing people and the accounting people, and order fulfillment people. You have an opportunity to learn some of their skills.

The advent of technology, the proliferation of e-commerce and e-everything means that you can always learn new tricks. Stay up on the latest software, keep abreast of the latest in your field, and then find a new aspect of the business to learn. Ask the people in those roles. Get training. Do whatever you can to have a resumé that gets longer every single day.

Give it Away

Your success is built upon the sum of your character's abilities. Sharing your skills and knowledge does not mean that you are putting your job at risk. Rather, you are bringing up the entire team, making everyone better, and making yourself even more indispensable. It can seem a little counterintuitive, working so hard to master a skill only to give away that knowledge to someone willing to learn. But that is how knowledge is passed down, that is, quite literally, how we learn. And you will find that giving away knowledge, teaching it to other people, often deepens your understanding of it because you begin to look at the things you know from a different perspective. I encourage you to seek opportunities to share knowledge with the same eagerness that you seek opportunities to gain it.

> *"Seek opportunities to share knowledge with the same eagerness that you seek opportunities to gain it."*

Who are the people around you today that have mastered a skill you would like to incorporate into your life? Who can benefit from the things you know how to perform? The only way we get better is to acknowledge that there's always room in our show for more.

Director's Notes *Choose one skill that is mandatory for your new character. Master it.*

DON'T LISTEN TO THE CRITICS

YOU WILL FORGET YOUR
LINES; IMPROVISE

DELIVERY IS EVERYTHING

BE BRAVE

SAY IT WITH ENTHUSIASM

BRING YOUR
PERSONALITY

LOOK HONESTLY AT YOURSELF

FIND YOUR VOICE

DEVELOP A STRONG, RESONANT VOICE

DEFINE YOUR CHARACTER

PROJECT
YOUR VOICE

If you met someone new right now, and they asked you to tell them about yourself what would you say? What would be the first thing out of your mouth? Would it have to do with your career? Your marital or parental status? Your age? What defines you? Or more to the point, what would you like to define you?

Actors have voices, those characteristics that define them; the attributes that make them stand out in audiences' minds. Jack Nicholson is rakish. Grace Kelley was lighter than air. Morgan Freeman lets you see just enough to know there is a whole lot more going on below the surface. Houdini was mysterious. Evel Knievel was fearless. But, I promise you, none of them started out that way; none of them knew their voice when they were breaking into the business.

Your voice is you, put forth for other people to hear. It is the projection of yourself. People with a strong voice are confident and comfortable in who they are. They understand the things that define their character, and rather than resigning themselves to those things, they immerse themselves in them. I think an example will help you understand what I mean.

A colleague of mine is the marketing director for Cincinnati Opera. He's good at it too. So good, in fact, that Chris was asked to teach at a local university about marketing for non-profit organizations. He was honored by the opportunity and started devising his syllabus immediately.

Chris called me while working on his plans for the upcoming semester. He was working diligently because he had never taught a college-level class and wanted to reach his students on a deep level. I reminded him that he was the perfect person for this job. I knew from years of personal experience that he was a gifted marketer and an innovator in his field. I told him not to try to be "Professor Chris"—that's not why he had been hired. He had been hired for his unique expertise and experience.

The point of this story is that Chris already had a voice. He had a strong voice, and the university recognized that its students could benefit from hearing it. At first, Chris thought he needed a different voice, one that sounded more like an academic or professor, instead of the one he already had. When he trusted his own voice, the class was a tremendous success, and Chris continues to advise colleges and arts organizations on marketing today.

Find your authentic voice

We all know people who say starting a company or making partner in a law firm or designing a building never seemed like work. They say they enjoyed the long hours and that they were willing to do whatever it took without complaint because they loved what they were doing.

How is it possible that these people exist in the same world as those who count the minutes on the clock in their cubicle? How can some people find so much satisfaction in their professional lives and others find nothing but frustration? It is not because the satisfied people are somehow genetically programmed for happiness, and the others are meant to be blue. It's because satisfied people understand their voice, they accept and embrace it and use it not only to project their character to the rest of the world, but also to guide their career and their decisions.

Having a strong voice is not about being loud or the center of attention. It's about having a clear idea of who you are, an inner monologue that dictates your choices. People with strong, authentic voices project them not through words, but through action.

Finding your voice requires a conscious effort. Ask yourself: Who am I? What about me makes me proud? What skills do I want to refine not because I think it will improve my resumé, but because I want to be the best at them? If I had a blank slate and the opportunity to create a whole new me for the world to see, what would I look like? What would I do? What would my relationships be like and who would I want to share them with? It helps to do this exercise regularly, to keep tabs on your voice. When a new opportunity comes up, measure it against your voice and ask yourself is this the old me or the new me?

Listen Actively

It's perfectly natural to feel frustrated. Many people are unhappy with something about their life: their career, their body, or their home life. They don't feel satisfied. They feel tired. They feel like a failure. And in a way they are. They are failing to listen to their own voice, the one that tells them to find a new job, to get to the gym, to work on their relationships. Your voice is two-fold. It exists as both projection and reflection, the thing we want the world to know about us and the thing that guides us through the world. Our voice sings, and its echo keeps us on track.

So what will you say the next time someone asks you to tell them a little bit about yourself? Well, you don't tell them all the things you are not. You tell them what you are, who you are, where you are going, what your care about and where you've been, and you will do it with a strong, clear,

"Our voice sings, and its echo keeps us on track. "

concise voice. You would gladly yell these things from the mountaintops, because it is the real you. Not the old you, not the one other people think you are, but the person you think of when you hear your own name.

 Director's Notes *When you wake up tomorrow morning, look in the mirror and see your new character. In your best, clearest, strongest voice, say your name.*

BE SPONTANEOUS
ACT WITH PASSION
PRACTICE
HAVE A SENSE OF PLAY
PLAY ANY ROLE
DON'T BE AFRAID TO BE FUNNY
HAVE AN IRON WILL
PASSION SUPERSEDES NATURAL ABILITY
STOP REHEARSING
YOUR LIFE
USE YOUR IMAGINATION
FULLY COMMIT

DO YOUR OWN
STUNTS

According to research released by the Nielsen Company, the average American spends four hours watching television every day. That's 28 hours a week, 1,456 hours a year. That means over a 74-year lifespan, the average in America, a person spends 12.29 years watching television uninterrupted—one sixth of their life!

That's almost the same amount of time it took to build the Panama Canal. It took less time for America to go from having no space program whatsoever to landing a man on the moon. If we are to extrapolate these numbers, we arrive at the astonishing figure of 445,231,195,136 hours spent watching television every year across the country. For anyone who has trouble reading that number, that's four-hundred forty-five BILLION, two-hundred thirty-one MILLION, one-hundred ninety-five THOUSAND, one-hundred thirty-six. That's time we're not using innovating, solving food shortages, curing diseases and generally making life better for the entire planet.

I'm not against television. I actually like it quite a lot. But television, like labels and old scripts, can be a crutch. We can become so engrossed in the latest reality television show that we forget we have lives to live. Some people prefer the safety of their couch to the possibility of getting hurt, physically or emotionally, in the real world. They hide; they shy away. They miss out on opportunities to learn and improve themselves, preferring instead to watch the lives of other people—fictional ones mostly—or retreat into the wider world of digital distractions—video games, the internet, and social media.

In short, they refuse to do their own stunts.

Doing your own stunts means facing the real world head-on, absorbing the good and the bad, enriching your character through the broad array of experiences the world has to offer and making your character stronger, wiser and more refined in the process.

Scars vs. Tea Cups

Here are two approaches to life that will help illustrate this point. There are people who confront the world and are better for having earned some scars, and there are people who hide, like a fragile piece of china, afraid of ever getting hurt and missing out on the full spectrum of human existence.

The people who do their own stunts are fully human. They are the nurse who changes bandages in the burn unit of a children's hospital, the people who work to help others overcome addiction, the men and women in the military, the people who stop to talk to the homeless. These are the people who drink life in. They are the ones who confront the worst the world has to offer with compassion and eagerness. They seem deranged to people who don't understand the richness of that kind of experience. They are also the people who are curious about the world around them and adventurous when it comes to trying things that are outside of their comfort zone. They skydive or talk to the stranger sitting next to them on the plane. They run headfirst toward life.

The other people, those who hide, are carried through life on one of those people-moving conveyor belts they have at the airport. They stick to what they know. They don't push themselves to try new things, to learn new languages or skills. And by limiting themselves to the familiar, they are automatically constraining their potential for success. They may interact with new people, but it's online. To paraphrase Dr. Will Keim, if you have 1,500 friends on Facebook or following you on Twitter, but don't have a date for Friday night, then you lose and should probably reconsider how you approach the stunts in your life.

Scars

There's an exercise I love to do with the groups I speak to. I call it Scar Stories. I gather people into groups of three or four and have them take turns going around the circle, telling the story of one of their scars. Sometimes the scars tell funny stories and sometimes they are sad. But there is always a story. Being able to tell the story means you survived. Your character made it through whatever experience created the scar and has a story to tell about it.

The fact is we all have scars. We all have things we've gone through in our lives. Some people hide their scars better than others, but we all have them.

I have a scar. It's on my index finger, and it reminds me of the first time I was ever asked to babysit. I was probably ten or eleven years old, and the woman in the apartment down the hall asked me to watch her daughter while she went out. As soon as the woman left, as soon as we were alone, the girl I was watching grabbed a knife and started running. I was terrified, shocked. I had no idea what to do. I grabbed the end of the knife and, as I did, she pulled it away and nearly took my fingertip with it. Not a happy story, but a true one. That scar reminds me to always be open with my children and attentive to their feelings.

It also was my last babysitting job.

The Nature of Scars

We all have scars, or at least we should. Scars are physical and emotional reminders of the things we have done, the things we have tried. If you are afraid of getting scars on the inside or out, then you are probably afraid to try. And so you put your life, like a precious cup, up on a shelf. You don't let anyone move it or touch it, you don't drink out of it, and it sits there for years, gathering dust and going nowhere.

There's a reason why we read about successful people like Richard Branson. If you don't know, Branson is the founder of the Virgin empire: Virgin Records, Virgin Airlines, and Virgin Galactic. He is a self-made billionaire famous for taking huge risks. Some people know him only for his stunts. He's an adventurer, a daredevil who takes on huge challenges like flying solo around the world and setting audacious goals like being the first private citizen in space. He holds world records for crossing the English Channel in an amphibious vehicle. He has crossed the Pacific Ocean in a balloon. He has attempted and failed to set the world record for speed sailing across the Atlantic Ocean and circumnavigating the planet in a hot air balloon. And, yet, he never gives up. He lives his life according to a code that calls for constantly pushing boundaries—in business and in his life. Unlike other people who attain a measure of success, he never rests on his accomplishments. He understands that there will always be more challenges and bigger experiences to be had.

"He doesn't do his own stunts because he is successful. He is successful because he does his own stunts."

It's not money that forces people like Branson to try daring things. He doesn't do his own stunts because he is successful. He is successful because he does his own stunts and always has. Trying new things, learning new things, stepping out of your comfort zone forces you to do more than just sweat, scream or be uncomfortable. Doing your own stunts forces your perspective to change. It forces you to have a broader awareness of the human condition. It gives you a wider view of the world and you are richer for the experience.

Stop Rehearsing Start Acting

Do your own stunts. Don't rely on other people to do them for you. Don't watch the reality show about losing weight—lose it. Don't just watch the show where people try to survive in the wild—do it yourself. Those people, those characters, are gaining from their experiences trying to light a fire in the rain while you, watching from your couch, are gaining nothing but a shorter, duller life with lower expectations and bigger pants.

What real-life experiences can you draw on that will make your character better? What have you done? What scar tells your story? Better yet, what are you willing to experience even if you acquire a new scar in the process?

Scars are not always physical, most scars involve our emotions. Emotional scars are often perceived as negative. They are thought of as handicaps. But if we fail successfully, emotional scars are signs of experience and risk-taking. They are the remnants of relationships that don't work out. But you can't be scarred from a relationship you were not invested in emotionally, and it's impossible for a relationship to truly succeed without emotional investment. So, isn't the risk of an emotional scar worth the potential benefit of a successful relationship?

Stunts don't have to be dramatic. I'm not telling you to run out and climb a mountain or bungee jump off a bridge. Doing your own stunts doesn't mean that you have to be an adrenaline junkie. Nor does it mean you should throw your television out the window and drive over your smart phone.

"Isn't the risk of an emotional scar worth the potential benefit of a successful relationship?"

Stunts are any act that requires an unusual effort. Maybe it's reaching out to the neighbor you have never met and inviting them over for a cup of coffee. You never know what you might learn from them. That person, who you would not have reached out to when you were acting out your old scripts, might be able to share wisdom and experience that helps your character evolve.

Of course the person might be mean to you. They may decline your offer or may not be the kind of character you want to cast in your show. You will only know by trying. You may end up with a scar and a story to tell or you may end up with a new character that had been waiting in the wings for their cue.

Stop treating your life like a dress rehearsal, a run-through the night before the big performance. Every day is a performance. We are promised yesterday but tomorrow is not a guarantee. Don't miss the opportunity to do your own stunts by putting it off for an uncertain future. Do them today and be ready to accept both the scars and the rewards.

Director's Notes *Think about a scar you have that was worth getting. Think about something that's potentially worth getting a scar to obtain.*

LEAP ᵒᶠ FAITH

It would have been easy for Towanda Williams to become a statistic—just another high school graduate from small town Mississippi, going to work at a factory, toiling every day and getting nowhere. It was what she, as an 18 year-old wanted. "My mom and dad asked me about college and I told them, 'no, no, no that's not me,'" she says. "I wanted to be a housewife and mom. That's what my mom did and that's what I wanted."

And she did just that. She went to work in the factory and got married. She had three daughters and settled into life in her hometown. Life was good for a while. But then she found herself divorced and raising three children on her own. She kept working, kept advancing and was proud when, at 41, she became a supervisor and put her oldest daughter through college.

But something wasn't right. She had done a good job. She had raised her children right and proved that she could be counted on at work. But her show was going nowhere. Her character was stagnant. She felt stuck and realized that no matter how much she enjoyed her job, her family, and coworkers, it would never be enough.

"I realized that I was losing opportunities by not having a degree," she says. "I interviewed for this job with the Chamber of Commerce organizing events and bringing groups to town. The interview went well, I really liked the people, and they really liked me. I was excited, and they were too, but then they asked me about college, and I had to tell them that I never went. The job required a college education, and they told me that they were sorry, but I wasn't qualified."

"I left with my head hanging low, and I promised myself that it wouldn't happen again," she says. She returned to her job, to the life she had built. To the town she had never left. But it all felt smaller. Staying where she was, she felt constrained. Experiences like the one at the Chamber of Commerce built up until one day she reached a tipping point.

"One day the spirit just came over me," she says. "I decided to go to college."

When Towanda says that the spirit came over her one day, she means it literally. She knew where she wanted to be and went there, driving from her home in West Point, Mississippi to the nearby Mississippi University of Women. It was one of those moments of absolute clarity. She decided to act, to seize the opportunity she finally realized she had. She found her way to the admissions office and walked right in to talk to a counselor. She soon found herself a freshman in college, joining the same class that her youngest daughter was enrolled in. She was the oldest student on campus, and perhaps the most determined.

She took classes at night after her shift ended at the factory, and after four years she was an academic junior having completed three years of full-time coursework in her spare time. She was chasing her dream. Then the news came that the company she had devoted 23 years of her life to, the company that had provided the livelihood that helped her raise her girls and put them through school, the company that had made it possible for her to go to college was closing.

"I got an e-mail from someone in human resources telling me that since I had already completed three years of school, the company would pay for me to finish," she says. It was, for this woman of deep and abiding faith, a "God moment." She felt like she was being watched over, taken care of. She never lost heart or considered another option. She didn't waste time fretting over what she would do next, but continued in the same spirit that got her off the couch four years earlier. She remained dedicated to her goals. She became a full-time student and completed a bachelor's degree in public relations in 2003.

Towanda's story would be a great example of how we are all capable of rewriting our shows, no matter the stage. Her story would be compelling if it had ended there, but it didn't. Not by a long shot.

After graduation, Towanda interviewed with a Memphis-based organization called the Southern Placement Exchange (SPE). A position as a Resident Hall Administrator at the University of Central Arkansas was open, and the people at SPE thought Towanda would be perfect for it.

So this woman, who five years earlier had a high school degree and a factory job, enrolled in a master's degree program, moving from her hometown for the first time in her life. She was branching out as a person, writing new scripts as she went, and serving as a surrogate mom to 180 juniors and seniors.

"I kept a picture of my girls hanging on the wall of my apartment to remind me what I was doing there," she says. "And I used to cook with my door open on Sundays. The students would come by, and we would talk about life. I would help them figure out what they were going to do with their lives, and help them keep on the right path. I fell in love with career services, helping people find their path."

Graduating with a master's degree in 2005, Towanda decided to return home. She started her current job with her alma mater, the Mississippi University of Women in the career services department. She helps students figure out what they are going to do with their lives. She is working on her PhD in organizational leadership and all three of her daughters are college graduates.

Towanda is 52 now and doesn't plan on slowing down. "It was time for me to do something. I loved my job (at the factory), but it was easy for me, there was no challenge and I think I just realized that I could do better," she says. "I like challenges. I like pushing myself and that's just what I did. I think I am proof that you can do it. I don't care what comes up; you can always achieve your dreams. I am living the dream."

The desire Towanda had to recreate her character is the same one that inspires each and every one of us to change. It is born of dissatisfaction. It is encouraged by dreams. Towanda can't be sure where she'll be in five years. But she can be sure that she won't be settling for what comes to her in life. She can be sure that she won't be sitting on the couch, wishing for something better. She'll be getting something better. She'll be making something better. Towanda Williams is just like every one of us. Change is possible. Improvement is possible. No matter what your age, no matter what you need to overcome.

EMBRACE YOUR CHARACTER

KNOW YOUR OBJECTIVE

STAGE FRIGHT IS COMMON

HIT YOUR MARK

TIMING IS EVERYTHING

BE IN THE MOMENT

ARRIVE WARMED UP

YOU WILL FORGET YOUR LINES; IMPROVISE

PROJECT YOUR VOICE

STAR IN YOUR LIFE

OPENING NIGHT

So you've worked hard on your new show, and it is finally the opening for this huge production you call your life. Every day you open your eyes is another opening for your show. Today, now, is the only stage of your life you will ever have control over—not the past, not what happened to you last week, or in the fifth grade. Where is your production today? Are you ready to make an entrance as your new character?

"Every day you open your eyes is another opening for your show."

Openings can be magical. It's the culmination of all your hard work. Do it right—hit your marks and nail your lines—and there is, in my mind, no greater feeling in the world. The audience applauds, a friend brings flowers, and you find yourself counting the minutes until the curtain goes up for another performance.

Getting Over Stage Fright

You may have spent months writing new scripts—envisioning your new character and lighting your stage—it's natural to feel nervous about moving forward. Your confidence may begin to fade while waiting in the wings. You may get stage fright, a very common occurrence. If you are not prepared, that anxiousness becomes fear.

Now is the time to remember what brought you to that theater in the first place. Why did you want to take your show to Performance Level? What changes and improvements were you hoping to make? Reassessing your goals and remembering why you made them can help you get over stage fright. The fear may not go away. You may still be anxious, but if you are confident in your decisions, that confidence will be enough for you to take the first step. And the second step is always easier.

Think about the entrance you make as your new character. What statement do you project before you ever say a word? It may be in a job interview or a parent-teacher conference, it might be the first time you see someone you know after writing your new character. If you are confident in that character, if you have a clear idea of who that person is and what traits and habits they embody, then projecting that confidence is crucial every time you make an entrance.

Opening Night Flops

So, let's say your opening night is a flop. What are you supposed to do? How do you cope when your show goes off script or you forget your lines?

You write new ones. You wake up the next day and make another entrance. You rethink your character and adapt.

For me, the best part of approaching your life as if it were a show in which you are its star is that the show will have a long run, and you will constantly be refining it, tweaking it and improving it until the day the final curtain falls. If you set a limit you are only inviting disappointment. If you say that you have to be the absolute perfect character by a certain day, you are limiting your show on the day after that. Goals need deadlines, but they also need to lead to other goals.

"Your life is a show and you will constantly be refining it until the day the final curtain falls."

We all suffer setbacks, no matter how carefully we

write our scripts. Outside forces—big forces like death and divorce—scripts beyond our ability to write or control, will force us off course. When they do, we have two choices: we can adapt and adjust—it's called ad-libbing—or we can remain paralyzed in our stage fright and berate ourselves for not predicting the change.

Greatest Flops

In over 30 years as a performer and speaker, I have had more bad performances, given more bad speeches than you ever have, simply because I've done both more than you. It is this experience of failure, I believe, that has led to my success and just to prove it, I thought I might share three of the biggest flops of my career.

Early in my speaking career, as I was trying to build a name for myself, I was hired to speak on a college campus as part of a monthly speaker's series. This was maybe my seventh booking, and I was pumped. No, not pumped, I was psyched. I couldn't wait to get up on that stage and give the speech of a lifetime. The person in charge of the speaker's series booked me months in advance for a date in January. For six months I looked forward to this keynote. I pictured myself delivering it perfectly, better than perfectly. I imagined myself holding hundreds, if not thousands of students hanging onto my every word. I counted down the days until my flight. I was flying!

My speaking career was taking off to the point that I was flying to an engagement. The day finally came, a Sunday night speech that would be the turning point in my career, a launching pad for my success. I arrived early and made contact with the person in charge of the speaker's series, who showed me to the hall where I was to speak. The time arrived, I stepped onstage and looked out over the room to see the most amazing crowd, one I absolutely had not imagined in the months leading up to that day. It was amazing not because of the overwhelming enthusiasm, but because of its underwhelming size. Three people showed up. Of course, I should probably mention that it was Super Bowl Sunday, something I wished someone had looked up prior to the booking, and the local team was playing in the game, which could not have been known at the time of the booking.

I remember thinking, welcome to Bombsville, population: me. I ad-libbed. I brought the students who made the effort to come up onstage, and we sat and went through my program together. I gave that talk everything I had and each student received a free copy of my book *Keys to Success in College and Life*, but it reinforced the notion that you have to be able to adjust when situations don't meet your expectations.

My second biggest flop came from my Marineland days. My performing partner Robert and I used to watch the high-divers at the park. We were amazed by their agility, the way they used their bodies almost without thinking. One day after watching them twirl and twist and spin, we both resolved to learn how to do a standing back flip. We pretty much decided that the ability to do a back flip from a standing position at the end of our performance at the dolphin show would make us the coolest people on Earth.

We had to learn.

We asked the divers—several of them gymnasts—to teach us and over the course of the summer they worked us out and held our hands, heads and shoulders. They gave us expert instruction. Soon, we were able to perform the standing back with little more than a diver's hand on our shoulders, like a parent teaching their child to ride a bike by running alongside and holding the back of their seat. In time, we were able to ride on our own, to do the flips without anyone holding on.

We were on top of the world.

During our breaks, we would go to a grassy patch near the lunchroom and do our standing back flips with enthusiasm. We were *The Men*. We were riding high and feeling cool, confident, and masterful. I guess that's why we were so willing, eager even, to help when a fellow Marineland employee, a 6 foot 2, athletic young man, asked us to show him how. Of course! Of course we could show him—we were experts, right? So we took him to the shady green lawn behind the lunchroom and demonstrated our technique. We told him the basics, how to thrust your shoulders back at just the right moment, tuck your legs tightly into your chest, stretch them back out and land gently on the grass.

He wanted to try. He planted his feet and took off. Robert and I watched his perfect leap, his perfect head-over-feet spin. We stood there and watched as his feet hit the ground perfectly and were a tad jealous when he nailed it on his first attempt. We stopped being jealous and got really scared when we realized we had not taught him to control his upper body on the landing. We got scared when we realized that we weren't holding his shoulders like the gymnasts had for months with us. We got even more concerned when we saw his face connect with his knee and the feeling of dread intensified when he stood up, gave us a funny look, and then spit his two front teeth and a long arc of blood onto the lawn in front of us.

To make matters worse, he was a trumpet player at the park. That was his first standing back flip and his last day working at Marineland. I never saw him again. So let me say now, from the bottom of my heart, I am so sorry. We had no clue how to teach someone else this new skill. I did fifteen or twenty more back flips in my life and never, ever, even thought about teaching someone else.

The moral of this story? Don't think you can teach someone else something in six minutes that took you six months to learn, just because it has become second nature.

But atop the list of Curtis Zimmerman's greatest flops, the number one all-time goof also happened when I was working as a mime. Every year, the city of Dayton, Ohio, has an outdoor festival called Downtown Dayton Days. It draws crowds downtown to the banks of the Great Miami River

> *"Don't think you can teach someone else something in six minutes that took you six months to learn."*

for music, entertainment, appearances by local celebrities, and speeches by dignitaries. I loved working Downtown Dayton Days as a performer. For one thing, I worked in the city long enough to know all the dignitaries and celebrities and most of the companies that sponsored the event and in turn, they knew and appreciated my work.

At the time, Dayton had a semi-professional soccer

team, and someone from the marketing department thought it would be a good opportunity for exposure if they asked the mayor to try and kick a goal while the news cameras were rolling. I knew the mayor and was working the crowd nearby while he tried. After he took his shot, and with the audience watching, he called to me, "Hey Curtis, come over here and try to kick a goal." The goal was made out of PVC piping and had been set up in front of the main stage and when I stepped up, I hammed it up. I was spinning the soccer ball on my finger, doing all kinds of miming moves and magic tricks, all gearing up for the goal kick. This was essentially center stage and I am an entertainer, so you do the math.

I hauled off and kicked the ball as hard as I could toward the goal, it never occurred to me that ball could veer off course, curve slightly, and hit the woman in the audience who appeared to be about seven months pregnant squarely in the stomach. I swear all you heard was a thud as I saw her falling backward and then I heard the rush of wind as every single person out there gasped in horror simultaneously.

It turned out that the woman was fine. She saw the ball coming and managed to get her hands up and, as far as I know, her child is in high school now, but the fact remains that often the biggest flops in our lives are the least expected. We have to be able to roll with the bad times and the good.

Be Willing to Improvise

If we are truly comfortable with the character we are playing, then we know how they will react to any unexpected situation. We're able to improvise when a supporting character forgets their lines. We can adjust when a piece of the set falls over or if there is a wardrobe malfunction. We don't lose our cool; we remain composed and move on, taking the next step toward reaching Performance Level.

Are you present in your life? If so, then you can act on the opportunities happening on or around your show, whatever stage of life you're in; you can adapt to flops and find new strengths within your character.

Having a clear understanding of what makes your character tick will help you step out onto the stage for opening night and it will help you get right back up when you fall. Keep your eyes focused on the back of the theater, keep your character moving toward a long-term goal. Don't let flops or set-backs ruin your show. If you are too rigid, if you only want to read exactly what is in the script, you're more likely to fall off the stage. If you stay nimble and remember that the path may change and there may be bumps, the goal never changes and you are more likely to stick with it when times are tough.

And yes, Downtown Dayton Days did hire me back the next year, but it's only because I didn't let one flop keep me from getting back up on stage. When you're in the midst of a flop, when you can feel the show unraveling and the audience growing restless, it can seem like the end of the world. But the lesson I learned, the truth that seasoned performers come to rely on is that there's always another day, another opening for our show.

Director's Notes *Tomorrow is the next opening for your life. Focus on that new opportunity and not on past or potential flops.*

Remind yourself what brought you to the stage in the first place.

ACKNOWLEDGE
THE AUDIENCE

ENJOY YOUR STANDING OVATION

SHARE THE STAGE

DON'T LISTEN TO THE CRITICS

A ONE MAN SHOW ISN'T PRODUCED BY ONE MAN

DON'T WORK FOR APPLAUSE

BE WILLING TO LAUGH AT YOURSELF

DON'T UPSTAGE

EMBRACE EACH MOMENT

TIMING IS EVERYTHING

TAKE A BOW

Life at Performance Level is an examined life, a life in which we are constantly evolving and improving. It's based on a desire to do better, be better, and play a better character with a better cast on a better set with a better audience.

Along the way, you will rewrite scripts and make casting decisions. You will change your character and improve. People will start taking notice. Maybe it's something you've done at work that merits congratulations from coworkers or a personal achievement like losing weight. People may pat you on the back and tell you how happy they are for you and your accomplishments.

In these situations, it is important to know

how to take a bow with respect, grace, and humility. It's also important to forget the praise the second you get it, the same way you should accept failure. Learn from it and move on.

Applause

People living at Performance Level don't do it for the applause—they do it for themselves. Applause is nice. Being recognized for your efforts can be a rewarding experience, but it should not be the reward for your experience. Your biggest reward should come from the satisfaction that you are that much closer, that much farther along in your journey.

> *"A good performer knows that taking a bow is an act of humility."*

Bowing is a thank-you for the audience's appreciation and a good performer knows that taking a bow is an act of humility. Sure, there are some talented people that may take the opportunity to bow as a means of gloating. But their stars fade fast. Great performers know that the real work continues long after the house has fallen silent and the audience has gone home. They know that the real test comes between performances. They understand the character they play offstage is as important as the one they play on it.

Taking a bow the right way requires three things: face your audience, bow with genuine appreciation and humility, and know that you earned the applause and that with hard work you can earn it again.

Face Your Audience

No man is an island. No one becomes successful alone. No show is without co-stars, stage managers, make-up artists and hundreds of other bit players that have helped you along the way. If you have ever been involved in performing, you probably know that the most significant people in your audience are your friends and family, the people you know and who know you. Facing them when you take a bow is a gesture of respect. It tells the audience that they matter to you.

Remember to share the applause with your supporting cast, because no great performance comes from one person alone. If, at work, you receive recognition for an achievement, it's vital that you share that recognition with the members of your team who helped along the way. If you receive congratulations on a wedding anniversary, it should be shared with your spouse, because there's no such thing as solo success in a relationship. After two decades together, my wife and I are celebrating our 40th anniversary because we both had to commit 20 years to each other.

Successful one-man shows always involve more

than one person. There may be a single actor on the stage, but an entire team of people are contributing by running the lights, helping with direction, costume and set design. Accomplishments, big and small, are rarely the work of a single person. There is no such thing as a completely self-made success. Even if you are the key to an achievement, there were other people who helped along the way and great performers always give thanks and credit where it is due.

Bow with Genuine Appreciation and Humility

If you are in a position to take a bow, chances are you have worked really hard. It's okay to be proud. Just as the opposite of love is not hate but indifference, so too, the opposite of arrogance is not the refusal to accept praise, but the inability to. I have met a lot of people who are humble to the point of denial. There is something about them so afraid of appearing arrogant that they deny themselves the ability to feel proud. Applause feels good. It feels good to be recognized for something done well, something for which you have sacrificed in order to achieve.

"Take your bow and be earnest when you do, but be ready to move on the second the applause stops."

It's all about balance. Pride without ego. Humility without apology for your success. Take your bow and be earnest when you do, but be ready to move on the second the applause stops.

Bow Knowing You Can Do Better

Arrogance is the belief that you don't have to or are not interested in doing any better. When you reach a milestone, when you achieve a goal, know that it is just one of many. Only a fool reaches a milestone and thinks it is a pinnacle. Don't be a fool.

There was a milestone early in my career that some performers might misperceive as a pinnacle. I was just out of high school, living on my own and working as a performer full-time. I had heard about the National Yoplait Mime Search and decided to audition. Yoplait was the yogurt of France. Mime was a symbol of French culture and the company wanted to use mimes as spokespeople. Yes, I am serious.

I looked around the audition and saw performers I had admired for years. We were given 10 minutes to do a skit and conduct an interview with Brad Pappas, the Yoplait representative putting on the contest.

I can still remember the feeling after I won. I hadn't even heard my name. I won $2,000 and a one-year contract to tour the country on behalf of Yoplait. I was 19 years old and had just been given a check almost too big to comprehend and an opportunity to follow my dreams. I celebrated in my car for about three minutes, and then it hit me—I still had to get up in the morning. I still had to go to work performing at Marineland. Winning had not taken away my responsibilities.

I toured as one of the Yoplait mimes for that year, but just as the contract was to expire, I was approached by Brad. He said he had seen my work ethic. He knew that I would be a professional, easy to get along with; I would show up every day and represent the brand well. He trusted that I would not let any amount of success or acclaim go to my head. He hired me that day, and I continued making appearances as the Yoplait mime for several years. For more than a decade after that, Brad and I continued to work together on other projects for other brands and other companies.

In all that time, I continued to refine my act and improve my skills. I received applause almost daily, and I took a bow every time. But I did so knowing that I would be right back at it the next day, with another performance, another crowd. I bowed knowing that if any of the people in the audience ever came back to see me, I wanted to put on an even better show.

Sometimes we let success go to our head. We get blinded by it, fooled by it. Yet, the most successful people I know never dwell on their success, they understand success means never settling for anything less than your best and knowing that your best can always be better.

Director's Notes *The next time someone pays you a compliment, hear it, smile, say, "Thank you," enjoy the moment, and get ready for the next scene.*

Make sure never to apologize for your hard work.

PUSHING THE ENVELOPE

Colonel Beale is a man unlike any other I have met and to describe him is not to do him justice. You have to experience him. Still, I hope the following story gives you an idea of the high ideal, strong work ethic, and sense of excellence this man has as the basis for his existence.

When you're flying upside down at 500 miles an hour, just 100 feet off the ground, there is a lot that can go wrong very quickly, and the results could be catastrophic. Add to that another plane flying equally as fast approaching from the other end of the airfield, preparing to pass just feet above you, and the situation gets that much more tense. The slightest twitch, the smallest misstep could result in death. The tiniest hiccup in your training, which was designed to override your natural instinct, and you are dead.

This was the reality for Air Force Colonel Michael "Mo" Beale when he was a soloist with the United States Air Force Thunderbirds performance team and what's more, it was not the highest pressure situation he found himself in during his nearly 30 years in the service. There were the escort flights over Bosnia, the times he was enforcing the "No Fly Zone" over Northern Iraq shortly following the first Gulf War, and the policy decisions he helped craft working for the Joint Chiefs of Staff. He could have gotten nervous, flinched when he was providing air support for ground troops on the fringe of the Iron Curtain in the early 1980s, or lost his nerve as a squadron commander along the DMZ in South Korea.

But that's not how Colonel Beale operates. That is not the culture in which he has not only lived, but also thrived for his entire adult life. His culture, the culture of the United States Air Force, and the military in general, is a culture of excellence, precision and dedication. His culture calls for the utmost in discipline, the relentless pursuit of a better version of yourself. It is a demanding world to live in, one in which only the fittest, the most able, the mentally toughest survive. It was the one he was born into, and the only one he knows.

Growing up on bases all over the world—his

father was an Air Force fighter pilot—Colonel Beale witnessed what it meant to be the best every day. And when the time came for him to make a life for himself, he chose the difficult and rewarding path of service. But first, he needed a haircut.

"When I went into the Air Force Academy I was 17, and this was back in the era of long hair. It was June of 1977 and the first thing they did was cut my hair off. I had a hard time sleeping, because every time I moved, it sounded like sandpaper," he says. The way he talks is precise, well intended, and humble. Even in talking about his youth, there is a certain amount of calculation to his tone, calm even in nostalgia.

At first, he thought he wasn't right for flying, that maybe he would work in the family business, but in a different department. "I used to get car sick, sea sick," he says. "So when I first started, I was pre-med. I wanted to be a veterinarian."

Unfortunately, the veterinary studies program at the Air Force Academy was cut, so he decided to change his mind and follow in his father's footsteps. "I enrolled in the pilot training program, and when you enroll, you choose between flying cargo, transport, or fighters. I went for fighters."

This is no small feat. Consider the fact that 700 of the 1,500 students in Colonel Beale's Air Force Academy class washed out, then consider that of the 65 students that applied for pilot training, only 32 were selected and of that 32 only six were chosen to become fighter pilots. You get a sense that anything he chooses to do, he does very well.

His first mission was at RAF Bentwaters in Eastern England, where he flew the A-10 Warthog, a lumbering, slow vehicle known for its toughness and reputation as a "tank killer." It was here that he provided air support for ground troops over Germany, toeing the line between East and West. "We were the first line of defense should the Warsaw Pact countries decide to attack." It was also there that he met his wife. "I was looking for an English girl. I was looking for Julie Andrews," he says. "I found better."

Supported at home by his wife and children, Colonel Beale served in situations of combat, like the missions over Iraq and Bosnia. He served in peace as pilot and ambassador with the Thunderbirds. He has been a policy maker at the Joint Chiefs of Staff and a strategy architect at Central Command. He has been an administrator, as Vice Wing Commander of Shaw Air Force Base in South Carolina. He has served in so many positions, played so many roles, but the one he found most rewarding was the one that brought him back to the United States from England.

In 1988, Colonel Beale was told to report to the small town of Enid, Oklahoma, for duty as a flight instructor. It meant leaving the aircraft he had flown for two years and abandoning a request for a duty in Asia. "I wanted to go to Korea and continue flying the A-10. I wanted to become the best in that aircraft as I could possibly be." He might have been disappointed, but he found teaching to be much more rewarding than he thought it would be.

"In all my years in the Air Force, teaching was the most rewarding experience. It turned out to be my favorite assignment of my entire career."

Teaching and learning are as big a part of life in the military as eating and breathing. Over the course of his career, Colonel Beale has earned four master's degrees. It should not be a surprise that education and imparting his knowledge meant so much to him. His mission as an instructor gave him the opportunity to be more than an educator—a mentor, imparting the knowledge and wisdom he gained in the classroom, on the tarmac, and in the air to the next class of fighter pilots, men and women to carry on the tradition of excellence.

Colonel Michael "Mo" Beale lives his life in excellence. He demands success from himself on a daily basis, and he offers those with a similar desire the assistance and expertise to meet their goals. He is constantly learning, and constantly challenging himself and pushing the envelope. He doesn't just live at Performance Level—he defines it. Every time he straps into the cockpit of an F-16, makes a life or death decision, or calls upon the past to guide his decisions, he is living the dream—his dream.

It's easy to look at his resumé—the Thunderbirds, the Joint Chiefs of Staff, the no-fly zones and master's degrees—and assume Colonel Beale is something "other," a person from a different kind of world. You would be wrong.

I know Colonel Beale. I've eaten dinner with "Mo" and his family, and witnessed not only his excellence, but also his thoughtfulness and heart. I've heard him talk about how much teaching means to him—from a man who defended our national security, challenged the limitations of gravity and stood bravely in the face of inconceivable danger. He is not as big of an exception as you may assume. Over years of working with military personnel around the country, I can honestly say that most are like him. They are "excellence-seekers" who understand that accomplishment and success are attributable to the team and to each person's knowledge that they can always be better.

It's the same with the other people I have written about in this book. Colonel Beale, Towanda Williams, Dr. Robert Evans, Rick Murrell and Roger Villarreal, these are all just people. True, they have overcome great hardships. But the biggest hardship they have faced is doubt and a feeling of being out of control. They are no different than any of us. We all have the power to do what these—and thousands of other people I have met over the years—have done, which is to realize that they are in control of their own shows. They have rewritten bad scripts and strengthened good ones. They have cast and recast their shows. They have succeeded with perspective and failed successfully.

They continue to live their dreams.

BE WILLING TO SACRIFICE

LISTEN ACTIVELY

COLLABORATE

DON'T BE AFRAID TO BE FUNNY

HAVE AN IRON WILL

TRUST YOUR GUT

GIVE YOUR SKILLS AWAY

LEARN ALL THE RULES BEFORE

YOU BREAK THEM

DO EVERYTHING WITH INTENTION

HAVE A SENSE OF PLAY

BECOME AN
ACTING COACH

Everything up to this point—all the script rewrites, the character improvements—none of it, ultimately, is for you. The reason we have focused so much attention on improving and starring in your show is so that one day, when you are ready, you can share everything you've learned with someone ready to learn it.

One of the greatest gifts you'll ever receive in life is the opportunity to share your knowledge. If you spend your career and lifetime learning, acquiring experience and the expertise to create an amazing show, the greatest thing you can do is give it all away. Your show will be far better if you help all the characters you meet perform at a higher level.

Encourage Imitators

Being a good acting coach is all about attitude. Some may say that they have spent a lifetime refining their character and working on their act, so why shouldn't up-and-coming performers, executives, and teachers have to do the same work and spend the same thirty years acquiring this valuable knowledge? I completely disagree with this line of thinking. This attitude halts the progress of the greater show. Let's say you have worked really hard to become

> *"If you spend your lifetime acquiring the expertise to create an amazing show, the greatest thing you can do is give it all away."*

a great architect and near the end of your career you create your masterpiece: a building of such fineness and beauty that you have truly taken the craft to the next level. The argument that your knowledge is yours alone means that as soon as the building is complete, you would have to knock it down so it can't be studied or serve as a way for people to learn, assuring no one could steal your creative genius.

Protecting knowledge in this way is something I see way too often. I have heard from more than one performer that I should not be showing someone else my techniques or my skills. They tell me others will steal my show when I am not looking.

Here's what I think: no one will ever perform one of my original pieces the way that I did. And because I am the inventor, by the time imitators have mastered the skills, I would have written and created something new. So, share your gifts whenever possible and encourage others to use everything that you have to make their show better. The truth of the matter is, that's what you did. You learned from others and incorporated their skills, tricks, and tips while becoming the person you are today.

Give it Away

Mentors share knowledge, wisdom, and experience that allow the human race to evolve and grow. If knowledge had been treated as exclusive to an individual, we would still be in caves, scrounging for our next meal. There would be no language, no culture, nothing of the world we know today.

Acting coaches, mentors, and teachers are the

"If knowledge had been treated as exclusive to an individual, we would still be in caves, scrounging for our next meal."

reason for progress. We all learn from those who went before us. So when you are asked to pass on your knowledge, you should approach it with vigorous enthusiasm. It is an honor. It is recognition of your accomplishments to be asked to help someone as they begin or continue on their journey. I have had the pleasure of sharing my experiences with several performers in my life. I know that I gained more from the experience of giving than they could have from receiving. The act of mentoring makes you realize that you teach what you most need to learn. You distill what was important from your experiences and pass on knowledge in its purest form.

My life has been blessed with great acting coaches. If it weren't for David Coleman, Dr. Will Keim, Tommy McLaughlin, and hundreds of other people just like them, who walked onto my stage and shared their gifts, my character would never have evolved into who I am today. My character is not perfect. I still have a long way to go, but I would have even farther to go if it had not been for these generous individuals taking an interest in my life.

Give it Back

Mentoring is my way of trying to pay back the people who mentored me. The gifts I have been given are immeasurable. The blessings are too numerous to count. And if I can just pass on some of that, if I can just make the slightest difference to someone who needs it, then I will know I have really accomplished something. My journey will have been made with purpose.

Receive it

But mentoring is a two-way street. The idea that a mentor is some sort of sage dictating wisdom to a silent, attentive audience is preposterous. If you are going to mentor, you have to open yourself up to the fact that you will learn from the person you are mentoring.

We all come from different places. We all have different experiences. Just because someone wants to learn from you, does not mean that in the future you won't be turning to them to learn from the skills they have mastered.

Mentoring is both an act of experience and one of deep humility, one that will make your character stronger. After all, what's the point of learning things, of adding skills to your repertoire if all you are going to do is keep them to yourself?

Your character has a temporary part in this world stage, but by mentoring and passing on all that you have learned, you leave the show stronger than it was when you made your first appearance.

Director's Notes *Who can you mentor? Look for people standing in the wings, hoping for a cue from you. Share something today to make their show better.*

STAGE FRIGHT IS COMMON
BE ON TIME
THE SHOW
MUST GO ON
ACT WITH PASSION
HIT YOUR MARK
KNOW YOUR PART
PRACTICE
KNOW THE END OF THE PLAY
KEEP AUDITIONING
IMPROVE YOUR
CONCENTRATION

TIMING IS EVERYTHING

Because producers, directors, and actors put time and energy into thinking through transitions, the world created in a show is plausible, believable, and engaging.

Although transitions can happen quickly, they take some of the most careful planning. Timing is critical for a smooth transition.

The same goes for your life. By now, you are thinking about changes you want to make to your character,

"Timing is critical for a smooth transition."

the plot, staging and arc of your show. You have set goals, identified old scripts, and are making progress toward writing new ones. But no show, no person can change completely in the bat of an eye. Dreams don't become reality overnight. That's why it is so important to consider timing and transitions to bring your life closer to Performance Level.

When I was transitioning from a career as a mime to one as a speaker, I knew I couldn't just quit one and move on to the other. I had to think it through. How was I going to get where I wanted to be? How could I continue providing for my family while making the switch? I knew my two careers—the one I had and the one I wanted—needed to overlap.

"Be comfortable enough to enjoy your current role, but uncomfortable enough to create change."

Transitions are tricky because they often require us to make extraordinary efforts to keep things the same and create change at the same time. We must be comfortable enough to enjoy our current role, but uncomfortable enough to create change. In an ideal world we would be able to simply change our minds, rewrite our scripts, and just like that, be the character we want to be. What a wonderful world it would be if all we had to do was close our eyes and visualize change. We could be whoever, whatever we wanted to be, without pain and hard decisions, without frustration or pushback from the characters that don't want to see us change. But this is not the world we actually live in. This is not the real world.

I live in the real world.

In the real world we have to overcome obstacles that stand in the way of the show we are performing and the one we wish to create. In the real world there are challenges and struggles, impediments to our happiness that must first be conquered. It takes sweat and discomfort to get to Performance Level. It takes hard work and dedication beyond what many of us feel capable of giving.

But we are capable. We don't give ourselves enough credit. Remember the room full of people who didn't believe I could teach them how to juggle? Remember the boy who grew up on food stamps and instability? We can achieve what we seek to achieve. The struggles, the hard work and sweat and pain and fear and uncertainty we fight through in order to get there, to achieve our goals and live our dreams makes arriving at that place, that new stage and new character that much more rewarding. It might be nice to inherit a fortune from your Aunt Mildred, but it wouldn't mean nearly as much as building a fortune for yourself.

We've spent a lot of time covering the evaluation of your current show, imagining your new one, and giving back once you have reached a goal. This chapter is all about the time between; it is about the middle ground between your life now and your life at Performance Level, your transition from one stage in life to another, and an old script to a new one.

Some changes are easy to make, in the short term at least. It isn't hard to say that you don't like a certain aspect of your life—a character in your show, a script that you believe is limiting your potential for development—and make a decision to change it. You stop calling that poisonous person that makes you feel like you are less than you really are or you decide to learn a skill that advances your potential. And that's great, but what do you do when that poisonous person continually calls you? What happens when you realize just how challenging learning something new can be?

If you don't prepare for these transitions in your life, it will be very easy to revert to your old ways, to answer the phone or give in to frustration. I know there were many nights when I wanted to give up on my dream of being a speaker; when I thought it would have been easier to just keep doing what I was doing and put aside the things I needed to build tomorrow so I could enjoy extra time with my family today.

This is what I mean when I say that transitions are tricky. The familiar is often more appealing or comfortable than the new. If you are not prepared to take on the things that can stand in the way of living the dream, then you will inevitably fall victim to reading old scripts.

Change will Come

Whether it is on purpose or thrust upon you, change will happen. And it can take two forms. First, you can change everything tomorrow; you can quit your job and tell the people in your show who are the most poisonous that you never want to talk to them again. This won't lead to a smooth transition. Your life will be turned into a violent storm, leaving debris, hurt feelings, and a path of destruction that will take years to rebuild.

Or, change can be managed. You can slowly give poisonous people fewer lines, allowing healthy people in the wings to step onto your stage. You can take down one piece of scenery at a time, as you create a new set, a new lifestyle. You can write new lines for your new character, give yourself new behaviors and parts to play over the next few months and watch your show materialize before your very eyes.

You didn't create the life you're living now over a weekend. I didn't develop the concepts of this book in one weekend. Rather, I have been working on them for the past ten years. Take time to enjoy the journey and before you know it, the lights, stage, characters, and plot will change dramatically.

 Director's Notes *Keep transitioning into your new role. Announce your transition to your supporting cast. Allow them to help you make a smooth transition.*

Remember, timing is everything!

STOP REHEARSING YOUR LIFE

ACT NOW

FIND YOUR LIGHT

ACKNOWLEDGE THE AUDIENCE

TAKE A BOW

STAR IN YOUR LIFE

STAND CENTER STAGE

EMBRACE EACH MOMENT

LIVE FULLY

GIVE YOUR SKILLS AWAY

BE BRAVE

PROJECT YOUR VOICE

ENCORE

Now that you understand what it is to live life at Performance Level, now that you know your dream and recognize it, what will you do? If a friend asks you what you learned, if they ask you what it means to think of your life as a great production, a masterful performance, what would you say?

"The life you live and the life you want to live are separated by only one thing—you."

If there is an overarching theme to this book, if there is a statement that wraps up all the metaphors, all the parables, it is this: The life you live and the life you want to live are separated by only one thing—you. An examined life, one in which you look at all the characters, the plot, the scenery, and the lighting, is a life lived at Performance Level. Once you realize that there is nothing standing between you and your ideal show, your dream, other than your own self-imposed limitations, a whole new world of possibility opens up to you. It certainly did for me.

I won't lie to you. I know that life can be hard. People lose their jobs and homes and hopes for a better life. We live in a world where people can easily spend their whole lives quietly desperate for something else, something more, something better. As cruel or stifling as this world can be, it can be equally beautiful, engaging, and exciting; it can be joyful and full of promise. This world, the world of satisfaction and reassurance is the real world as well.

"The only difference between light and darkness is a person's willingness to turn on the switch."

It would be easy to get philosophical, to talk about the light and the dark, the good and the evil, the yin and the yang, and I promise not to do that here. I will say that the only difference, many times, between light and darkness is a person's willingness to turn on the switch, to open the blinds and let light into their life. Good and evil are separated by the intentions of those who realize they have the power to choose.

Choose

You have the power to choose. I hope you understand that. I hope I have made it clear that your life is largely up to you. You can choose to dwell on the bad things that have happened to you, and we all have had bad things happen to us, or you can choose to take negative experiences for what they are—opportunities to learn and grow, to add depth to our character, or intrigue to our plot. But it takes a certain mindset, a posture of confidence, a way of being in which you choose to overcome those bad things and dwell in the world of the positive. Negative experiences, however horrible and scarring, are not permanent. That is, unless you allow them to be. If you allow negativity to be your crutch and spend your whole life holding onto it as tightly as you can, then you will never know if you can walk on your own. Let it go. Let it all go. All the things that have prevented you from reaching your Performance Level, all the things you have allowed to cloud your vision and impede your dream—let them all go. Give them up to God, to the past, and to the former version of you.

The Show of a Lifetime

Now is the time for you to make a choice between the life you have and the one you want. Now is the time for you to find the resolve to do whatever it takes to put on the show of a lifetime, your lifetime. Now is the time for you to decide that you deserve your dreams, you deserve to have the things you want, to be the person you want to be, whether it is President of the United States, the world's greatest mom, the CEO in the corner office or the entrepreneur in the corner store. Make your choice. Make it happen.

What is that choice? Only you can decide. Only you can be the architect of your dreams. But ask yourself: What are you willing to do today, right now, at the end of this chapter to make it a reality? What sacrifices are you willing to make? How many miles are you willing to run? How many classes are you willing to take to find reality in your dreams?

There are two promises I am willing to make when it comes to helping people live their dreams: First, it will be hard. Second, you can do it. It will be hard because people in your life may be resistant to the changes you begin to make. It will be hard because anything worth having is. It will be hard because dreams and great shows require sacrifice and a willingness to get back up after rejection, to find your path again when you have been misled, to stand tall in the face of adversity.

You can do it because you have made it this far in this book. There is something inside of you—a voice, a vision, a feeling—that is telling you you're not fully content where you are. Listen to that voice, pay attention to that vision, that feeling, and allow it to be your guide. It may not take you down the straightest path, but it will get you to where you want to be. It may take time; you may not rewrite your scripts or refine your show to the point of Performance Level until the day before you die, but how wonderful it would be to leave this earth knowing that you got to experience something so many people never have, if only for one day! How gratifying it would be to achieve that point of perfect contentment, of satisfaction, even if only for a fleeting moment.

Be patient, but don't settle. Be diligent and never lose sight of that point on the horizon, that place of achievement. During your journey, be mindful of others. Remember that they are on their own journey as well; they are starring in their own shows. Remember too that we are all in different places on the path from Point A to Point B, from birth to death, from our present life to living our dream.

Also remember that the only person who will be completely dedicated to your life, the only character in every single scene is you. Ultimately, it is your responsibility to put on your show. It is your dream that you are after, your dream that you want to live. Other people will be involved, characters will share scenes—some more than others—and plots of different shows will cross over, merge, and diverge again. But at the end of the day, when the house lights come up and the final curtain is drawn, it will be your story that will have mattered. Make it the show to end all shows.

Now, it's time for you to start living your dream. Put down this book and get out there! Get up on stage and stand front and center. Belt out a song. Nail your lines and hold the audience in the palm of your hands. This is your time. Now is the time to go after the things you want. Now is the time to open your heart, your mind, and stage to the people who love you and who you love.

I look forward to seeing you out there on the stage of life.

Acknowledgements

A one man show is not produced by one man.

There are many people whose love, knowledge, time, and support helped make this book a reality. Walt Disney said that "all your dreams can come true if you have the courage to pursue them." Each one of you has given me such courage.

I thank…

God for being the one true source of light in my show.

Craig Heimbuch for all the late night sessions allowing me to verbalize my concepts, for your time and patience with my process, and most of all, for your friendship. You are my "Brother in Christ."

Jeni Sand for your ever positive, "get-er done" attitude. Thank you for always keeping this project and me on target.

Chris Milligan for sharing your multitude of gifts with me. You always positively challenge my pace and perspective. You are a great friend.

Nate Cooper for sharing your Cirque family with me. You are an amazing artist and I am blessed to call you friend.

John Galvin for the brilliance.

Darryl Levering for engineering the brilliance.

Aimee Sposito Martini for adding your creative flair to so many projects throughout my career.

Diane Ness, **Don Frericks**, **Chris Milligan**, **Jeni Sand**, and **Michelle Zimmerman** for taking the first peek and giving me your constructive feedback.

Matthew Kelly for your guidance and mentorship, allowing me to become a better version of myself. I am proud to call you a colleague and friend.

Diane Tenaglia for your humility and sensitivity toward my written word.

Roger Villarreal, **Rick Murrell**, **Dr. Robert Evans**, **Towanda Williams**, and **Colonel Michael "Mo" Beale** for sharing your hearts with me in such an open and honest way that I felt the world needed to hear your stories. Thank you for the honor of allowing me to present your stories to the world.

My wife, **Michelle** for all your love and project-managing support. I love you.

My children, **Noah**, **Mirabelle**, and **Oliver** for all the sacrifices you made during this process and for teaching me what it truly means to love unconditionally, that rewriting scripts can be fun, and that I can learn a lot from Lego building, duct tape creations and princesses.

My audience for allowing me to share the last ten years with you defining and refining my message.

Acting coach

A mentor. A person who will share their expertise with you.

Ad-Lib

Going off script. Adapting, adjusting, and improvising in the moment.

As-if theory

The practice of intentionally embodying the behavior, language, and wardrobe of the character you want to become.

Authentic voice

The unique projection of yourself. The characteristics that define you.

Casting Director

As the leading character, you cast the show by selecting characters that will support, love, provide comic relief and insight to your production.

Character skills

A unique set of abilities and knowledge a character may need to possess to reach Performance Level.

Co-star

The person who plays the biggest supporting role in your show: your spouse, partner, family member or friend.

Costume

The clothing and accessories that support your character's role.

Debut

The first performance of a new production or show, also known as an opening. Every day you open your eyes is "opening day" for your life.

DNA

Do Nothing Average.

Director's notes

Suggestions from the show's director given at the end of every rehearsal for incorporation into the next performance. Specific notes at the end of each chapter to help the reader apply the concepts of this book.

"Do your own stunts"

Facing the world head-on. Absorbing the good and the bad, and enriching your character through the broad array of experiences the world has to offer.

Failing successfully

Embracing and celebrating failure as a means of learning a better way to achieve a goal.

Flops

An unsuccessful scene or production. You've rehearsed and prepared a great show but it still bombs, leaving questions about what to do next.

General wash

A warm glow of light that covers the entire set and stage.

House Lighting

Lighting that illuminates the entire theater prior to the beginning of the performance and during intermission.

Improvisation

Acting in the moment in response to one's immediate environment and inner feelings. See also **ad-lib**.

Lead

The main character in your production. YOU!

Light of examination

A focused light that provides an honest assessment of your performance.

Light of possibility

You are born with an internal light. In that moment, you are capable of anything humanly possible.

Light design
Creating specific lighting to set the mood and tone of your show. The goal is for your character to flourish in the atmosphere that you create.

Mastery
Learning and rehearsing a skill until an extraordinary level of accomplishment is achieved.

Natural ability
Gifts and talents acquired at birth. Your natural skill set.

New script
Re-writing an old script by changing how you respond, how you act at any given moment, where you choose to go, and how you choose to get there.

Old script
Limiting thoughts and/or beliefs that hold you back, tear you down, and tell you "no." Old scripts create automatic responses without regard to your current reality.

Opening night
The culmination of your hard work. Your debut.

Passion
Your natural skill set taken to the outer limits of your limitations. Passion supersedes natural ability every time.

Performance Level
The act of striving toward a better, more developed life with the goal of meeting your own aspirations and achieving your own vision. It is the highest, most polished degree of excellence an artist can achieve.

Projection
Confidently putting forth your voice and vision.

Real-sumé
Your life story. The unique characteristics that make up who you are (not found on your résumé).

Set design
Surrounding yourself with tools, objects, and accoutrements that complement and reflect the nature of your character.

Script
A powerful force, thought or belief in your life ingrained in you from your past. Scripts can be stifling, empowering, good, or bad.

Supporting character
People you surround yourself with including family, friends, coworkers, and colleagues.

Taking a bow
Accepting compliments and applause with humility and genuine appreciation.

Typecasting

Assumptions made about us or by us based
on inaccurate or incomplete information.
Snap judgments that limit our perceptions of
other people.

About the Author

As a speaker and author, Curtis Zimmerman has impacted over 1 million people around the globe with his life-changing message. He expertly accelerates culture change, energizes organizations and creates greater accountability to keep companies competitive and focused.

Audiences connect with Curtis through his high energy, interactive style, and approachable manner. He incorporates the skills he gained from over twenty-five years in the entertainment industry into his powerful programs. Zimmerman is a highly sought-after speaker among Fortune 500 Companies, the United States Air Force, national trade associations, universities, and non-profits.

He is the author of *I Believe...What do you Believe?*, *Keys to Success in College and Life*, and a contributing author to *Pillars of Success* and *Lessons from the Road*.

Curtis currently resides in the greater Cincinnati area with his wife and three children.

curtis zimmerman
group

We at the Curtis Zimmerman Group believe that individuals and corporate bodies can rewrite what we call "scripts" and can learn to perform at a higher and more balanced level. We believe that the integration of personal and professional responsibilities is essential to human happiness.

To find out how Curtis can impact your organization visit:
www.curtiszimmerman.com
513-229-3626

LIVING THE **DREAM**™

To see and learn the skills that Curtis has acquired over his 25 years as a performer, check out his video blog and over 150 how-to videos!

www.livingthedream.tv